Witchcraft Guide

A Modern Guide to Witchcraft with Moon Spells, Rituals, Herbal Power, Crystal Magic, and Candle. Create Your Own Magical Life
(2022 for Beginners)

Don Law

TABLE OF CONTENTS

INTRODUCTION

Witchcraft was once considered a myth. Not at the moment. Not anymore.

Witchcraft does not simply exist in today's world; it thrives among the masses. To whom are we referring when we speak of the masses? After all, we don't see many witches on the streets of New York, unless they're cosplaying.

While it is true that few witches are visible in public, this does not mean they do not exist. Not all witches dress in black, with hairstyles that appear to defy gravity and eyeliner that is so dark that it could absorb all light.

That is not to say that gravity-defying hairstyles and black eyeliner are unattractive.

However, the public perception of witches is that they are outcasts.

Even though the majority of witches choose to conceal their practises, they do not regard themselves as outcasts. They do not, however, avoid society. They do not lock themselves in a dark room devoid of light and festooned with enough witch décor to serve as the setting for the next Exorcist film.

They are all around us.

Indeed, many witches are quite forthright about their beliefs, preferring to interact with others and form bonds with like-minded individuals. If you peruse the vast universe of the internet, you are certain to come across groups of witches that host regular meetings, events, and activities. Individuals are welcome to join them and learn about their world.

What are these witches exactly? Are they followers of dark magic and ominous entities? Do they concoct potions in a large cauldron using strange ingredients such as elephant toes and a gecko's tail in order to win the lottery?

Not even remotely close.

Today's witches are thoughtful, intelligent, compassionate, and community-minded individuals. Many of them hold steady jobs and participate actively in cultural and societal activities. Witchcraft is not a devolution of human belief; it is a return to the days of superstition. Rather than that, one could consider it an evolution of human beliefs; a forward step, if you will.

Witchcraft is far more relevant in the modern world than many of the world's religions. It emphasises social and individual responsibility. It acknowledges that the universe contains mysteries about which we are unaware and that we should raise our consciousness to higher levels. Several concepts ingrained in the witchcraft religion include respect for nature, equal rights for all, planetary stewardship, brotherly and sisterly love, and familial bonds. Yes, witchcraft is a religion, and not simply because some people believe in it. It is because the United States courts declared it to be so in 1986.

When most people read the preceding, they are taken aback. They do not anticipate witchcraft to be that progressive. What they do not realise is that witchcraft is a way of life that broadens our horizons regarding the planet we call home, the people we interact with, and ourselves.

With this newfound awareness of witchcraft's ways, a large number of people become "Seekers," or those seeking to adopt a witch's lifestyle. How does one become a member?

That is the issue.

If you wish to join the Christian faith, you are probably aware that your first step should be to approach a church. For Muslims, their faith is symbolised by a mosque; for Hindus, it is symbolised by a temple dedicated to a specific god. When it comes to witchcraft, there is no official organisation that regulates membership. If you're looking for information to help you better understand the religion, you've come to the right place. However, if you are looking for ways to join it, you may come to a stalemate.

Witches congregate in groups called covens. The majority of these covens remain wary of new members, and thus do not simply open their doors and spread the red carpet for anyone. Who is to blame? Witches are still discussed as if they were a new species of mole rat.

The thing is, witches who are members of covens are delighted to dispel popular misconceptions about them. They are eager to assist you in your quest to decipher the religion. Entering the coven is a different story.

Out of sheer frustration, the majority of would-be witches end up founding their own covens or going solo. When this occurs, these witches frequently experience a sense of being "out in the woods." In other words, they vanish. They are unsure of which sources to consult in order to gain an understanding of witchcraft, frequently relying on any or all available sources. This becomes quite dangerous, as they may not always rely on reliable sources. Additionally, there are numerous covens that base their beliefs on strange rituals sprinkled liberally with Satanism and Voodoo. With such strange practises, witchcraft frequently earns a bad reputation, and new witches are frequently duped into false practises.

Witchcraft is an extremely "liberal" religion. It does have some fundamental tenets and ritual patterns, but unlike other religions, it does not have rules that are specific to various aspects of life. This is why witches are able to diversify their practises. Consider witchcraft to be a river. It follows a path from the summit of the mountain to the sea, which it eventually connects to. However, the river can branch off into numerous tributaries along the way. The same holds true for witchcraft. Each of the tributaries represents the various covens that exist today, each diverging from the "mainstream" of beliefs but following their own path.

This is why individuals embarking on their journey into the world of witchcraft require their own guide. They will be able to comprehend witchcraft more fully and with the correct information after reading this guide. This guide can assist these individuals — or a newly formed coven — in practising their beliefs in a manner consistent with witchcraft's values. Additionally, it enables individuals to easily join covens by possessing knowledge on a par with — if not better than — that of any of the coven members.

Christianity is divided into several denominations, including Roman Catholic, Protestant, and Methodist. The same is true of witchcraft. While navigating the religion, you may come across various denominations.

Just as one form of Christianity is not appropriate for everyone, one branch of witchcraft is not appropriate for everyone. However, it is precisely because of this that witchcraft is exemplary. Each of us is unique. Each of us is a product of a unique culture and ethnic background. We navigate life according to certain principles and general guidelines.

Witchcraft is a personal journey. It's about bringing out the best in you while also teaching you to respect yourself, others, and the world at large. It is similar to the journey one takes when practising yoga in that it is both spiritual and magical.

While this book is primarily intended to serve as a guide, you can also think of it as a witchcraft course, one that will walk you through numerous facets of the religion and instil the necessary knowledge.

With that in mind, there is a great deal that we will learn together. After all, I will be guiding you in the capacity of a friend. Consider the act of reading this book as your first coven membership.

You will gain sufficient wisdom to embark on your own path and either become a witch on your own or find a true coven that is meant for you.

Welcom in de wereld van de witchcraft.

Blessings of light.

CHAPTER 1:

BEING A WICCAN AND BEING A WITCH

This chapter is intended to assist you in determining which category you will fall into if you begin practising witchcraft on a consistent basis. The terms witchcraft and Wicca, as well as the term "witch," are frequently used interchangeably. It can become confusing, so this section is intended to help you better understand the various labels and terminologies, so you can continue to develop your own sense of what it means to practise witchcraft.

To begin, witchcraft is a worldview and set of practises associated with rituals believed to "harness and focus cosmic psychic energies in order to effect desired change."

These actions and practises are collectively referred to as magic. Modern witchcraft, as it is currently defined, appears to be the largest subset of Neo-paganism, which literally translates as "new paganism." The majority of those who practise witchcraft in the United States, approximately 600,000 people, identify as Wiccans. That is, they practise Wicca as a religion. In 1985, the United States officially recognised Wicca as a religion, and it has since branched off into several other subsets.

Often, the distinctions between the smaller branches of Wicca are negligible. Alex Sanders founded Alexandrian Wicca in 1960, and it is frequently confused with traditional Gardnerian Wicca. Their differences are in the names of the tools they use, the deity and elemental games they play, and minor differences in the rules governing what is required to perform certain rituals.

Algard Wicca was founded in 1972 as a synthesis of Alexandrian and Gardnerian Wicca.

Dianic Wicca is a strictly feminist tradition born in the United States that places a premium on the Goddess rather than the Gardnerian tradition's constant emphasis on gender polarity. (In traditional Wicca, the union of a male God and a female Goddess is celebrated.) This branch of Wicca is particularly concerned with the

12

plight of women, and takes a very female-centered approach to all issues that arise.

Druidic Wicca holds the belief that all of nature is divine in some way and that everything in nature is interconnected. There is little information about the rituals and magic used, as Druids have historically maintained their history solely through oral communication. They incorporate a greater element of metaphysics into their traditions and beliefs than the original Garderian Wicca does.

Solitary Wicca is the type of Wicca that the majority of people practise in the modern world when they first become acquainted with and drawn to the religion. Clearly, as implied by the title, this is a form of Wicca that is practised alone, without the aid of a coven; a coven is a group of witches who practise spells and rituals together and gather at key times of the year on the Wiccan Calendar. This is almost certainly where your journey will begin if you choose to identify with the fundamental beliefs of Wicca (which will be listed later).

Eclectic Wicca is defined as the practise of one's own Wiccan traditions or the incorporation of other traditions into one's own. This branch of Wicca does not strictly adhere to a single set of rules in practise.

Now that you've learned about the various Wiccan traditions, it's time to discuss witchcraft and how it relates to, or is not related to, being a Wiccan. Because this book focuses on spells and magic (both of which are spelled with a 'k' in the Wiccan religion), the concept of being a Wiccan will exist independently of these actions. Witchcraft is precisely that; the actions that utilise specific tools to attempt to exert influence over energy and outcomes in our daily lives. Certain individuals who practise magic, belong to covens, or participate in rituals do not refer to their activities as witchcraft, as they dislike the negative connotations associated with the term 'witch' and its historical connotations. That is also true for those who do not wish to identify as witches; the term may be too ingrained in popular culture references for an individual to feel comfortable claiming it.

Others use the term witch to reclaim a title with such a negative connotation; they take pride in their title as witches because they are living proof that the beliefs and assumptions about witches were incorrect.

Thus, it is not necessary to be a Wiccan to practise witchcraft, nor is it necessary to practise witchcraft to be a Wiccan. Many people who do not practise witchcraft do not refer to themselves as witches for this reason, but still adhere to the fundamental beliefs promoted by Wicca. There are numerous forms of witchcraft that have inspired, and continue to inspire, people outside the realm of Wicca and its subsets. Indeed, the fact that there are so many other variations of Wicca, non-Wicca witchcraft, and forms of Paganism adds to the allure of forging one's own spiritual path, simply because it is not predicated on a rigid set of rules to follow.

CHAPTER 2:

UNDERSTANDING WITCHCRAFT

WHAT QUALIFIES AS A WITCH?

There is no one else on this planet who can tell you if you are a witch except you. As I mentioned previously, witchcraft encompasses a wide variety of practises and beliefs, and if you identify with any of them, you can identify as a witch. That being said, I understand how difficult it can be to determine whether you are truly a witch or simply enjoy the culture. As I previously stated, many people do not consider themselves witches, but rather Wiccans, and you may be unsure whether this is your path or if you are a witch. I'll outline the characteristics of a witch and the signs that you might be one below.

15

You can also look into your past or childhood (as I have), and you're likely to come across an instance or two in which you were in touch with your witchy side.

Witch characteristics

Witches have a strong connection to mother nature. They enjoy being outside and are able to sense a spiritual energy when surrounded by nature. They also have a strong spiritual connection to the moon and may even feel drawn to it on full moon nights. Witches have a strong affinity for animals and plants, which frequently results in them being vegetarian or vegan. Witches who consume meat or processed foods frequently experience sluggishness or a draining of their energy. This is especially true following fast food consumption.

Witches are acutely aware of the energy present in a space or with another person.

They are extremely sensitive to negative or positive energy. Witches frequently experience an overwhelming sense of energy (either positive or negative) when near a location with a long history, such as an ancient ruin or an old house. Additionally, they sense a very strong energy when in the vicinity of a cemetery, a war zone, or another location with a history of death.

Due to their sensitivity to energy, witches are extremely empathetic and even emotional. Witches have a strong sense of a person's energy when they are in pain. Hospitals can be extremely overwhelming for a witch. He or she will pick up on the energy of the hospital's residents and may even burst into tears for no apparent reason. Witches have a reputation for being irrationally emotional.

This is simply because they can pick up on other people's energy and thus may cry or become upset even when they have no reason to. This instils a strong desire in witches to assist and heal others, which is a significant reason for them to practise witchcraft. The majority of the time, it is for the healing and well-being of those in their immediate vicinity.

Witches are human, and while they appear to be like everyone else, they know they were put on this earth to accomplish more than the average person. As a result, witches may always have a sense of being unique or different from everyone else. This is frequently very noticeable during the childhood and adolescent years. They have interests that are distinct from those of their classmates and frequently seek out alternative films, books, music, and hobbies.

If a witch is unaware that she is a witch during her adolescent or early adult years, this will cause a great deal of frustration and anger. Teen witches who are unaware they are witches will experience a great deal of teen angst, whether they express it publicly or privately. Once the witch begins practising witchcraft, this frustration and inner struggle will subside.

Symptoms of witchcraft

The most frequently occurring indicators that you are a witch.

- You have an overwhelming connection to nature, which encompasses animals, the environment, plants, and the cosmos.
- You sense the presence of a feminine goddess, particularly when the moon is present.
- You have premonitions or come true dreams.
- A keen interest or curiosity in all things occult and magical

- You have the power to manifest your desires and influence the universe. Consider the case where you are thinking about a friend and they text you. Alternatively, you've forgotten your wallet and a friend offers to pay for dinner without asking.
- You feel a sense of obligation to assist and heal others. You wish to alleviate human and animal suffering.
- You dislike your doctor and are on the verge of abandoning conventional medicine. You even avoid taking Advil or cough medicine, preferring to heal yourself with teas or other natural remedies.
- You are aware of the seasons and intuitively recognise when they change. You can smell the change in the air and feel the temperature change much more quickly than anyone else.
- You sense the energies of crystals and are drawn to them. You enjoy the way they look and feel.
- You notice indications. You are able to decipher symbols or signs and deduce the message they are attempting to convey. This could include the perception of cloud formations, symbols, or specific numbers.
- Observation of ghosts or spirits. This may entail seeing them physically or simply sensing their presence.
- You're interested in alternative lifestyles; you're not a fan of the conventional.

There are numerous additional indicators that you are a witch, but these are the most prevalent. You do not have to feel all of these, but if you are truly a witch, you are likely to experience at least a few of them. Bear in mind that the only person who can determine whether or not you are a witch is you!

Practical Mysticism

According to some, magic and the occult are a very mysterious exploration of elaborate and secret rituals that are only visible to coven members. Others regard witchcraft as a "once in a while" activity that induces a "witchy" and mystical feeling.

On the contrary, practising witchcraft has practical applications in our daily lives and can significantly benefit anything we do.

Your awareness of how it works and how to use it will help you understand that when you apply the ritual of magic to all aspects of life, not just the grand celebrations or the intense and dramatic rituals, you gain a tremendous amount of energetic influence toward whatever it is you are attempting to accomplish.

There are literally thousands of spells for every conceivable need and desire. You can use magic in your craft to boost your career potential or ascend to the position of boss in your field of work. You can create spells to keep your home free of negative energies and vibrations. You can create rituals for bedtime and dream induction. You can even perform spells to boost your vitality and energy.

Practical magic is magic that can be used for anything and everything, particularly the small things in life that require an extra bop on the head from your wand and broomstick. You can begin to comprehend this reality the more you practise with the tools provided by the Craft. If you have a wonderful idea for something you want to happen in your life, you can manifest it magically through your spells and rituals.

Regardless of how you wish to practise, it can be a very reliable source of empowerment if you embrace what is necessary to infuse your life with a little more magical oomph. People all over the world use magic on a daily basis, developing methods to make an offering to whatever they value most or are attempting to manifest into reality. The Craft is analogous to casting a line to the great divine and informing the entire Universe of what you wish to do, be, receive, let go of, and become.

Consider how you would prepare a simple soup for dinner or how you would water your garden. It's comparable to cleaning your home or organising your garage's tools and equipment. While creating magic is undoubtedly more enjoyable than the mundane tasks we all face, consider how it gains greater meaning and impact when applied practically.

Empowering Your Own Personal Strength

Much of magic is about self-empowerment. There are numerous religions that emphasise the selfishness of empowering oneself or choosing to enrich one's life by becoming the divinity of one's own world and reality, but the truth is that when we are all in divine connection with ourselves, we empower everything in a much more positive way.

You may view it as a personal spirituality if you wish, and as you continue to practise, your journey with the Craft will assist you in discovering and uncovering your deepest, truest self and purpose. Numerous spells and rituals that you perform can be extremely strongly linked to your personal gain, which is a good thing. You will work to establish connection and gratitude with the energy of all things in order to achieve balance, which will benefit your personal empowerment even more.

The most effective way to assist yourself in achieving success in your own life is to devote energy, thought, and devotion to it. Your spiritual work possesses a tremendous amount of life-force energy, and regardless of what you are working on in your life or incorporating practical magic into, you will manifest a reality of personal success and triumph as a result of your desire to manifest it and demonstrate to the Universe what you desire!

It's such a creative and enjoyable way to connect with your wisdom and inner strength. There is a reason why so many witches were persecuted and burned at the stake in the past: their personal power terrified people. At a time when people were expected to be financially secure and devoted to a single male god, the majority of women and some men who practised witchcraft were powerful individuals capable of undermining the practise of other, more "important" beliefs and religious practises.

The truth is that each of us possesses a distinct inner power, and in today's age of technology, social media, and competition to be the "best" at everything, we become lost in a vast sea of pretending to be someone we are not. When you practise the craft, you are concentrating on yourself or whatever object you wish to work with magically, and you are listening to your inner path and power.

It is what will bring you into alignment with your highest self and lead you to the life you truly desire, not the one you are pretending to enjoy for the sake of "fitting in."

Consider what you need to bring into your life as you look around. Investigate ways to strengthen your own magic and true purpose and make them the focal point of your Craft. You can offer blessings and gratitude to the great divine for pointing you in the right direction, but magic is highly personal and will assist you in finding the best path for YOU.

Therefore, Let It Be Mote!

There are numerous proverbs in the Craft that can assist a witch in putting a period at the end of a spell. With a few simple words, you can truly propel your purpose into existence. Words are loaded with meaning and power, and as you peruse the various spells in this book and other sources, you will notice that there is a poetry to casting magic.

You are not required to be a poet or even a good writer to come up with your favourite words or phrases. You can simply state what is clear, direct, honest, and true in order to communicate your magical purpose and message to yourself and to the rest of the world.

"So mote it be" is a phrase that is frequently used to conclude your regular incantations. This phrase will appear frequently in the spells contained in this book, and It Is also likely to appear in a variety of other witchcraft resources. "So mote it be" is a declarative phrase that means "this is what is occurring" or "this is my truth, and there you have it." "And thus it is," is a frequent variant of this phrase. This conveys the same idea of enveloping your magic in truth and declaring that it already exists.

The words you use in your magic and crafting are critical because they are what carry your message through all things' energy. The language you use to express your purpose will be most effective if it is direct and straightforward, rather than overly descriptive, convoluted, and uncertain.

When you are unsure of what you want to say, simply consider what you are attempting to manifest. You can visualise the outcomes in your mind and visualise them as if they already exist.

Even if the words are not spoken, the energy of your intentions can be felt through thought or vision and carried forward through your magic. And all it requires at the conclusion is a single phrase to hammer it home: Thus shall it be!

Taking Care of What Needs to Be Done While Causing No Harm

The greatest challenge for all witches is to avoid creating magic that will intentionally cause harm or pain to another being, regardless of whether that other being is a creature, a plant, or a tree. Because the energy of all things is intricately connected, there are aspects of making magic that present difficulties when attempting to avoid harming anything.

Often, the resources required to perform magic are derived from our physical world. We gather materials and items through harvesting, wildcrafting, or purchasing in order to have the tools necessary to cast. At times, cutting a bushel of herbs for your apothecary cabinet can feel as if you're harming something; a living plant that deserves to be here just as much as you do.

According to the principles of magic, as long as you are not causing harm to anyone, you should continue with your magic. I've discovered that the best way to ensure I'm not causing any harm is to inquire. I always check with the plant before harvesting any herbs from my garden or from the wild. I describe my intent and purpose, and almost always receive a direct message from the plant or flower.

The key to understanding magic is to look beyond what the physical world has taught or demonstrated is real and to act in accordance with the spirit's laws in all things, including the rocks and stones you may collect for your altar. You'll desire to perform magic, and it must be done; the trick is to do so without causing any harm. You can see how speaking to a rosemary bush may appear insane to many people, but are those individuals regularly practising magic?

When it comes to people, extreme caution is required. You certainly do not want to bring unnecessary karma into your life, and even if you are bitter and rejected as a result of being dumped, this is not a good reason to hex someone. The better course of action would be to create a ritual of letting go of that person and to aid your recovery through the magic of self-empowerment rather than vindictive retribution.

You are not required to think about other people while working on your craft, unless you have their permission. You can create magic with good intentions and communicate with the energies present in all things to ensure that your craft is on the right track. If you approach magic from this perspective, your energy will respond significantly better to the magic you create. Communicate with the world around you, seek permission, explain your cause, and direct your magic toward empowering yourself rather than disempowering others.

Connecting to the Divine in Everyday Life

Witchcraft is an incredible way to connect with the divine in everything. Working with practical magic enables you to delve into another dimension of reality and illuminate these greater forces.

For many Wiccans, choosing between the Goddess Moon and the God Sun is straightforward; however, other Pagans and witches will choose from a much larger pantheon of cosmic deities who have been discovered and named over time and each represents a distinct reality or life energy. These energetic life forms give meaning to our individual crafts and can infuse our practical practises with a greater sense of purpose and truth.

When beginning a ritual or spell, or when casting a circle of protection, a general rule of thumb is to humbly express your gratitude and thanks to the energies or deities that you are summoning, thanking them for their presence in your work and connection to your magic.

Whether you feel their presence or not, when you incorporate and invite this intentional energy into your rituals, you invoke a greater sense of purpose.

When you invoke another source of energy to assist and assist you, your energy is enhanced. It is a necessary component of the way magic is crafted. We are all in this together, and regardless of how you choose to view and incorporate the source energy of something into your life practise, when you connect to the divine, you will have a greater light shining through all of your magic.

Witchcraft requires a willingness to view the world with more open eyes, greater wisdom, and intuition. All of these answers are available when you look within and learn from the ancient, hidden magic that resides there. You were born into the modern era, but your forefathers and mothers passed these universal truths on to you, and your connection to the Craft exists and will always exist within you.

Witchcraft is all about recognising the rhythms of your life in relation to the world around you.

After-Death Existence and Reincarnation

While the cycle of birth–life–death is self-evident to everyone, for many witches, the cycle does not end there. Rather than dying with the body, they believe that an individual's soul, spirit, or personal energy travels to a realm beyond the physical and will eventually reincarnate in another body at a different time and place. Many of them regard the earth as a "school" and believe that humans are here to learn. This cycle is repeated until the soul has absorbed all of the lessons it set out to acquire. Once the cycle is complete, the soul retires to a state of joy and regeneration.

Of course, this is not a unique concept to witches. Christians, Muslims, and adherents of numerous other faiths believe that our souls continue to exist after our bodies die, while Hindus have believed in reincarnation for thousands of years.

Where Do Witches Go After Death?

Christianity has its own version of heaven. Nirvana is a concept in Buddhism. Where do witches go after death? Many Wiccans believe that their souls travel to the Summerland, a place of rest before being reincarnated into new bodies in an eternal cycle of birth, life, death, and rebirth.

Harmony with the Earth

Witches understand that we are interdependent with the earth and that it makes sense to engage in practises that benefit both. "Every step we take is on sacred ground," some witches sing. They seek to live in harmony with all of nature and to restore balance to energies that have become out of balance in our technologically advanced society.

We frequently refer to our planet as Mother Earth, and she is indeed our mother. In some ways, this means that everyone and everything on the planet is a part of a vast extended family. When you recognise your connection to a greater whole, it becomes more difficult to act in opposition to that whole. This would be counterproductive and would be detrimental to your family, friends, and yourself. Witches make a conscious effort to move gently, to respect all life, and to recognise the sacredness inherent in all things and in one another. If we are successful in this, we will be able to heal the earth, and the earth will heal us.

Green witches in particular follow this path. Certain witches may work to protect endangered lands and wildlife, believing that their loss would be a crime against Gaia (one name for the earth's spirit; goddess of the earth in Greek mythology). Others donate money or volunteer their time to environmental causes, and they frequently send out positive energy via spells and rituals. Later in the course, you'll learn how to contribute to greater health, peace, and wellbeing in your own region of the world and beyond.

CHAPTER 3 :

MEDITATION FOR THE MODERN WITCH

Meditation is frequently associated with specific activities in contemporary society, such as yoga. And this makes sense, as meditation has historically been associated with yoga and other similar practises. However, regardless of one's preference for yoga, the practise of introspection and ensuring one spends time with one's own mind is something that anyone can do. And if it is something that every magician should do.

Meditation's Purpose

Meditation, or mindfulness as it is sometimes referred to, is the act of searching within for peace and calm. Many people, myself included, struggle to find this in today's world. Indeed, there has never been a time when the majority of people were adept at

28

establishing their own tranquillity. And modern life is so fast-paced that it's difficult to believe we can keep up. However, we can. You certainly can.

The exercises below are an excellent way to begin your meditation practise. It's possible that you'll have to repeat them several times before they become effortless or even productive. It all depends on how difficult it has been for you to look at your energy fully up to this point. Meditation is not without its difficulties. It compels you to take an honest look at yourself. However, it will bolster your magical practise more than anything else.

A Fundamental Grounding Exercise

Grounding is the first and most critical skill that a witch must acquire when working with their energy. Grounding lays the groundwork for the remainder of your magical acts. If grounding your energy sounds like something out of an electrician's manual, you're not far off the mark. When you ground, you extend a portion of your energy into the ground and use this taproot to syphon off unwanted or uncontained energy. Additionally, it will enable you to more easily wield energy from a higher power, as you will be able to channel excess energy into the ground.

Naturally, your grounding point does not have to be the actual ground.

Depending on the source of your energy, you may wish to ground to the structure of a building or the ocean floor. You may even ground to the vast stillness of space if that is the source of the majority of your energy.

However, you should begin by grounding yourself into the earth beneath your feet. To begin, you'll want to sit on the ground

29

and close your eyes. Find a comfortable position and concentrate on releasing all tension from your body. You can begin with your fingertips or toes and work your way up.

You'll want to maintain tension in your core to avoid injuring your back. However, ensure that you release tension around your eyes, across your temple, and in your mouth. Additionally, your shoulders will store stress, and you may need to take a few deep breaths to relax them.

Once the tension has been released, it's time to check in on your breathing. Inhale as deeply as possible without rushing or attempting to take a deeper breath than normal. Count the seconds it takes to complete this, and then hold your breath for two to three seconds.

Exhale slowly and deeply until your exhalation takes one to three seconds longer than your inhalation. Throughout your grounding practise, whenever you become frustrated or lost, return to your breathing and release any accumulated tension.

Concentrate on your breathing for approximately a dozen breaths, then shift your attention to a mental image of yourself. It can be as realistic or as fantastical as the author desires. Once you've established the mental image, visualise a taproot of your energy burrowing into the ground from the base of your spine. Alternatively, visualise a network of roots burrowing down from every point on your body that makes contact with the floor.

If you are on the second – or higher – floor of a building, you can either visualise your energy flowing through the floors beneath you to the ground. Alternatively, you can maintain your focus entirely on your mental image of yourself and visualise yourself sitting directly on the earth to facilitate grounding.

Burrow as deeply as is comfortable for your root or roots. Then, once you feel secure and connected, begin channelling all of your negative energy into the ground. This will channel the energy into the earth, where it will be cleansed before being returned to the world for new purposes. You may continue doing this for as long as you wish, alternating between focusing on your breathing, your tension, and the movement of your energy. Although it may not appear so, this is the most fundamental form of energy manipulation, which is a necessary skill for all witches. And, once you've mastered this technique, you can progress to centering.

A Fundamental Centering Exercise

Grounding and centering are frequently discussed in the same breath. However, they are two distinct practises with distinct objectives and outcomes. And as such, they can be carried out independently. You should ensure that you understand how to ground, at the very least on a fundamental level, before proceeding to centering.

If you move directly from grounding to centering, you can use the same mental image that you used for grounding. However, if you are centering without first grounding, you should create a new mental image. In either case, your mental image should include threads of your energy emanating from you and connecting to each location where you expend energy.

Certain individuals perceive their energy as shimmering lines of a colour that they believe reflects them. Others imagine their commitment lines to be black cords, chains, tethers, or even strands of tinsel or fairy lights. You may even discover that different commitments have connections that appear to be unique to them. There is no single way to view your connections because, as I previously stated, magic is extremely personal and unique to each individual.

After visualising all of your commitments, it's time to evaluate them. Proceed through them one by one, ensuring that you approve of each connection or that you are required to leave them in place. If you wish to terminate the connection, you can disconnect your energy from the recipient and return it to your core. If the commitment is lengthy, you may need to cast an additional spell to permanently cut ties with the recipient. Additionally, many connections require routine action to completely sever. However, centering is a good starting point for determining which connections require this level of attention.

If you choose to maintain a connection, ensure that it receives only the energy it requires. Certain connections may require a significant amount of energy. However, there are others, such as groups you are forced to join regardless of your wishes or a job that does not reward employees for going above and beyond, in which you do not need to invest much energy. If you have these types of connections and are unable to cut them, you can apply a throttle or brake to them to avoid wasting energy in areas where it is not required or appreciated.

Proceed through each connection one by one. Each one that has been disconnected can be rolled back into your core and absorbed into your available energy pool. If you grounded yourself prior to focusing, you can cleanse this energy by channelling any unwanted remnants of the recipient – or your feelings about them – into the earth.

Centering enables you to ensure that your energy is spent wisely. This is an excellent practise for all users of magic. However, it forces you to examine yourself and how you spend your energy.

You may discover that you devote your energy to causes you do not truly believe in or that you spend as much energy as you do.

Examining yourself this closely can be challenging. However, you will discover that knowing yourself more fully elevates your magical practise – and your life in general.

Magical Meditations

Along with grounding and centering, there are numerous other meditations that can help elevate your magical practise. Many of these meditations are guided less by an external force and more by the path your own thoughts take.

A frequent misunderstanding about meditation is that you must empty your mind of all thoughts. That you must think only of white noise in order to meditate effectively. However, this is not true. Concentrating exclusively on white noise prevents you from being aware of your own thoughts or exerting control over your own energy. Plus, our brains are not wired for silence. Even when we are sleeping, our minds continue to communicate. Dreams assist us in processing information gathered throughout the day and in working through issues that concern us.

Our brains are perpetually active.

Meditation is no exception. You are not required to completely clear your mind. And you may discover that you are unable to clear your mind in the manner in which you believe you should. Rather than that, you must learn to allow your thoughts to come and go as they please. When attempting to learn something about yourself or a situation, you may choose to concentrate on or follow a single thought. However, you must allow the remainder of your thoughts to pass by without attempting to hold onto or dwell on them.

33

However, meditating in order to discern information is slightly different. If you want to use your meditation to learn something – about yourself, about situations, about spirits, or about the people around you – you should enter your meditation with a specific thought in mind. Concentrate on what you already know. Then, once you've regained your equilibrium, you can follow this thought and see where it leads.

When you work with magic, the fascinating thing about thoughts is that they take on a life of their own. Numerous spells are fueled by intention, which is nothing more than highly focused thought. To that end, you will notice that your thoughts take on a life of their own when you work in magical environments or attempt to perform magical acts. This has the potential to be both a blessing and a curse.

Active thoughts may draw your attention away from a spell or divert your attention from your meditation. However, they can also serve as an inspiration for creativity. Or, in this case, they may assist you in acquiring new skills. When you direct your thoughts toward yourself and the hidden aspects of your mind, this is called Shadow Work.

Do not be fooled by the name. There is nothing inherently dark about shadow work, except that you are examining objects that do not normally see light.

However, this is not necessarily a bad thing. Shadow Work is best left to witches with some experience and a firm grasp on their energy. Having said that, it is a necessary step in the majority of magical journeys. When you are ready to begin shadow work, you may discover that it evolves significantly more than you anticipated.

Everybody has aspects of themselves that they are not fully prepared to confront. We have unresolved old memories, bad habits, or toxic connections. And the majority of people can go their entire lives without confronting these issues directly. However, as a magician, you are not like the majority of people. The further along your magical path you travel, the more critical it is for you to address these characteristics or shadows.

Without confronting your shadows in your magical practise, you leave yourself vulnerable to negative energy. Furthermore, it can result in energy drains, preventing you from reaching your full magical potential. Therefore, begin with grounding and centering. However, when the time is right, do not be afraid to follow your thoughts and delve into your shadows.

Spells of Protection

Protection spells are, in a sense, a witch's bread and butter. They were the most frequently requested spell when magic users became more involved in daily life. And they will almost certainly consume the majority of your energy. The world is perilous. However, when you have control over the flow of your own energy, you can eliminate some of the uncertainty.

Self-Protection

Your magic is an incredible weapon. It is capable of a great deal and can bring about a great deal of change. However, it is first and foremost an extension of yourself. As a result, it's natural that you'd use it to defend yourself.

Magic is most effective when used in conjunction with other energy-based attacks or dangers. With the right kind of magic, negative spirits, other magic users who attack you with magic, and people who suck away your energy without realising it can all be stopped in their tracks.

If you have additional concerns about your personal security, you may want to consider other options. Magic is a means to an end, not a panacea, and should be treated as such. And, when it comes to personal safety, it is best not to take chances.

While there are numerous spells available for self-defense, I prefer the mirror spell. It requires only a sense of grounding and centering, as well as some visualisation. You will only need to find a quiet location where you will not be disturbed while visualising your protective barrier. Once it is installed, however, you can perform periodic checks to ensure that it remains strong without having to devote as much time to it all at once.

And, while it is necessary for you to be familiar with your grounding and centering exercises, you are not required to be an expert before attempting this spell. Indeed, it is one of the first spells that new users of magic should learn. True, it is merely a tool in your arsenal. However, on your magical journey, you will come across a variety of strange energies and entities. Additionally, it is always prudent to be prepared.

To begin this spell, find a comfortable place to sit. As I previously stated, you will need to devote considerable time to visualisation the first time you create your protective mirror. Therefore, it is prudent to cast this spell while in a comfortable position. Additionally, you may wish to inform the members of your household that you require some alone time. Though they are not required to tell them what you will be doing specifically if you are not open about your practise. Notifying them that you require some time is one way to ensure that you are not interrupted until your visualisation is firmly established.

As with any other spell, raise your protective wards or circle. Then reposition yourself in the most comfortable position possible. Close your eyes and perform your grounding and then centering exercises. Both steps should be taken slowly. This spell is for your benefit and well-being. Thus, being extremely deliberate and precise with your grounding and centering is an effective way to keep your mind in the proper place.

When you ground, be certain that your energy is securely anchored. Additionally, take the time to ensure that your foundation is truly compatible with your energy.

This book's grounding guide is geared toward earth witches. However, there are numerous options available. Whatever provides you with a sense of permanence and security is a good thing to ground yourself in, as long as it is not another person. As I previously stated, always ground yourself in something greater than yourself so that you can trust it to support you.

When you are ready to centre, spend slightly more time than usual identifying the direction of your energy. Take time to consider each connection and ensure that it is something you desire. Remove the connection if you do not want it. And, if you do decide to keep it, make certain that you only provide it with the energy it requires. We frequently want to give our all to certain things, such as family or passionate endeavours. That is perfectly acceptable. However, certain activities, such as work or group commitments, require a certain amount of our time. When we give more and are already stretched thin, we receive a low rate of return, which can leave us feeling drained.

Draining your energy reserves is one way to expose yourself. That is not to say that you should invite negativity into your life or anything similar. However, negative energies can detect when our defences are weak and attack at those times. When your energy levels are low, you will also become vulnerable to more mundane stressors. Things that you would normally shrug off become intolerable, which can result in additional problems.

Therefore, carefully consider your connections. And if you discover that some of the connections you wish to completely sever require mundane action, make a mental note to take care of them as soon as possible.

After you've completed both the grounding and centering exercises, direct your attention to your mental image of yourself. You used one for your centering practise; you can use the same one for this visualisation exercise. Concentrate on one part of your body at a time, beginning with your feet. As you do so, visualise yourself being encased in a sheet of armour. This may sound oppressive, but remember that this is your visualisation. You can design the armour to be as light and breathable as you like without jeopardising its durability or effectiveness.

Your armour must also be reflective, which is why Mirror Armor was created.

This reflective surface will reflect negative energy back at the source. You may feel their negative energy in the same way that you would feel a blow through armour. However, you will not be directly affected by it. And that can make all the difference when confronted with a situation or person that is intensely negative.

This is also why it is critical to progress slowly through the visualisation. When I perform this spell – and I have done so several times because, like real armour, it must be refreshed periodically – my mental images resemble something out of an old cartoon. Flashing lights and stirring music accompany me from head to toe as shining armour nearly mythical in appearance outfits me. As you might imagine, these images take a considerable amount of time to complete. However, this is time well spent. Finally, when I open my eyes, I feel secure and content in the knowledge that I am protected from any negative energy that might come my way.

Your visualisation will almost certainly be different than mine. That is a positive development. Everyone has something about them that distinguishes their energy signature from the energy signatures of those around them. This distinction is what synchronises your spells with you. And, in this case, it is precisely what will contribute to your armor's effectiveness. No energy can pass through your armour unless it is specifically designed to benefit your unique energy signature.

Visualizing a coat of armour from your feet up will take some time. However, as you can see, the time is well spent.

Begin with your feet and work your way up slowly, paying special attention to joints and areas where movement would cause clothing or armour to wear thin.

Even psychic armour – another term for what this is – will eventually deteriorate due to the natural wear and tear of life.

When you reach the summit and complete a full suit of armour from head to toe, envision sinking into your skin. This does not cause pain or discomfort. Rather than that, it should feel cosy and inviting, like your favourite sweater or the moment just after you slip into a warm bath.

Take a moment to express gratitude to the higher power with whom you work. You and the energy source both invested a significant amount of energy in your armour.

Gratitude and expressions of gratitude will go a long way toward ensuring that your relationship with your chosen energy source remains positive.

Open your eyes and take a moment to reacquaint yourself with your surroundings. This may take a brief moment, depending on the duration of your visualisation. When you are stable, expand your circle and re-enter the flow of everyday life. You may

39

experience fatigue, hunger, or dehydration. This is completely normal after exerting so much control and energy. It is critical for your health that you consume a snack, drink some water, and rest. Avoid performing any additional magical work on the same day as you set your mirror armour, as this will leave you dangerously depleted. As a side effect, your secondary spell will be weaker than it would be if you rested for a day.

As previously stated, you will need to reapply your armour on occasion. However, if you check in once or twice a week – something you can incorporate into your centering practise – you will be able to identify any weak spots in the armour before they spread. Additionally, you should check in if you are going through a particularly trying time or dealing with a particularly negative person. When you discover a weak point in your armour, devote the same amount of energy to mending it as you did to creating it in the first place. While this level of personal protection is strenuous, it is well worth the effort.

Protecting Your Residence

Some of the earliest forms of witchcraft can be traced back to protective spells and enchantments. These took the form of magical talismans, door frame carvings, and prayers etched into the very foundations of a home. The majority of modern people no longer have easy access to their home's internal structure. However, there are numerous ways to cast a protective circle around your home.

Witch jars are based on a number of these ancient practises. Rather than burying a single enchanted item beside your front door or at the entrance to your garden, you collect a collection of small items and place them in a jar. Following that, the jar is buried in place of the single item.

The following items are frequently placed inside witch jars:

- Nails
- Thumbtacks
- Thorns
- Pins for sewing
- shattered glass
- Pottery that has been broken
- CDs that have been damaged
- Knives de cuisine ancienne
- Screws

If it is sharp and poses a threat to you, your household, or anyone inside, you can place it inside a witch jar. You simply need to find a jar large enough to hold the items but small enough to fit outside your front door or beside your front gate.

After you've gathered all of the pointed objects in your witch jar, it's time to add the stinging ingredients. These are liquids or spices that would cause excruciating pain if injected into a wound. Several popular choices include the following:

- Vinegar
- Juice of Lemons
- Pepper
- Cinnamon
- Flakes of red pepper
- Ginger powder
- Wasabi

If you do choose to use acidic liquids such as vinegar or lemon juice, keep in mind that they are acidic. They may react poorly if you choose to use broken CDs. Additionally, any liquid will corrode metals submerged in it over time. If you notice that the protection spell has waned over time, it is possible that your more corrosive ingredients have corroded. You'll need to unearth the original witch jar and recreate it.

Witch jars are incredibly simple to assemble. Additionally, because you are working with your entire home's energies, you do not need to raise your wards, ground, or centre prior to creating one. Once completed, bury it near a common entry and exit point to your home. If you leave it out, the protective energies may fade and drift outside your property lines, as they are not anchored in the ground upon which your home is built.

Some readers may find the concept of a witch jar unsettling. After all, it appears as though the magic is intended to cause harm. And, while many witches employ curses and hexes without hesitation, some may be uncomfortable with such magic. If you are one of these individuals, you can rest assured that this spell is not intended to cause harm to specific individuals. It is not a calamity.

Rather than that, a witch jar functions as a warning system. It will deliver a mild "sting" to anyone who attempts to harm those who live in your home. It functions similarly to a mirrored protection spell, in that it returns a person's energy to them. However, the witch jar has the added layer of "sting" to deter someone from repeating their actions.

CHAPTER 4:

GUIDE OF SPELLS WITH CANDLES, MOON, CRYSTALS, AND HERBS

Flame magic is the most straightforward form of spellcasting and in that capacity, it does not necessitate an abundance of lavish ritual or instruments officiels Anyone who possesses a flame has the ability to perform miracles. When did you last recall Prior to blowing out the birthday candles, you made a wish cake. A similar argument could be made for light magic, except that

You're pursuing your willingness to work out according to plan stating your objective in a straightforward manner. Generally speaking, the birthday candle ritual is beneficial is predicated on three enigmatic critical criteria:

- Fix a goal.

- Consider the outcome.
- To demonstrate that outcome, centre your objective, or will.
- Candle Selection

The majority of experts on enigmatic frameworks will tell you that Your flame's size is truly irrelevant. Perhaps monstrous candles are appropriate counterproductive. For instance, a three-day-old light Consumption can be extremely distracting for someone who is casting a spell. which requires the flame to burn as long as possible.

Generally, a slight dimming of the light or the use of a votive candle will suffice. Occasionally, a spell may require a specific perspective, for example. For instance, a seven-day spark or a figurative flame can be used to communicate with a particular person unique, a form of considerate magic. Among the most celebrated In all honesty, the candles are the small menorah candles sold in boxes throughout the supermarket's entire vicinity. They measure approximately four inches in circumference white, unscented, and slender in length. They're ideal in this regard.

Work of spells

You should always burn a brand-new candle straight from the package not candles used at the supper table, but candles specifically for spell work or the previous day in the restroom. As some mystical sources indicate In accordance with conventional wisdom, a candle receives vibrations from the objects in its immediate vicinity.

It immediately ignites. If a pre-used candle has been tainted by waves, Individuals believe it will elicit a supernatural event that is contrary to or insufficient result.

Colors of a Candle

In terms of colours, you might want to keep a selection on hand for numerous enigmatic reasons. Typically, flame-related colour messages As follows, magic is as follows:

Red symbolises bravery and well-being, as well as sexual desire and love.

Pink is a colour associated with friendship and tender love.

Orange: Both a source of attraction and solace

Gold: Financial growth, entrepreneurial endeavours, and solar energy associations

Yellow: The colour of assurance and persuasion.

Green: Prosperity, abundance, and wealth

Health, toleration, and comprehension are symbolised by light blue.

Dark Blue: Suffering from depression and a lack of power

Purple symbolises aspiration and strength. Activities involving the earth or animals are darker. Negativity and eviction in the dark

White symbolises innocence and truth*.

Silver is associated with meditation, intuition, and the lunar cycle.

* It is worth noting that a white candle is sufficient in numerous Pagan rituals rather than a different hue.

Utilization of a Candle in a Ritual

After you've selected a candle, oil, or other preparation for use, it's time to light it a strategy for establishing telepathic communication between you. Likewise, the sun. You are providing energy to the flame and individual vibrations and anticipating your intended entry into the wax It is employed by you.

To dress a candle, you'll need some essential oil; numerous experts recommend the following:

I prefer grapeseed because it is completely odourless.

Additionally, to employ various flame magic oils obtained from a mystical source stores.

Rub the oil down beginning at the highest point of the candle centrally located. At that point, begin at the candle's base and rub it in a circular motion oil in the direction of the centre, concluding with the final pertinent point of interest. The blessing is performed in the polar opposite manner in certain rituals in the following manner; begin in the centre and work your way to the two ends.

If your project necessitates the addition of herbs, roll the oiled candle in them until it is completely covered in powdered herbs. This is critical. That candle, however, is merely a tool. Naturally, it is not. enchanted; however, it is a method of generating magic through the use of the component. of fire to motivate oneself toward a goal. Likewise, as various Instruments are employed in accordance with the nature of the extraterrestrial objective.

To avoid this, candles should be thoroughly cleaned before use. for the duration of your stay. The simplest form of light magic involves the use of a scrap of shaded paper. which serves as a focal point for the flame's purpose. Decide on a subject. Determine what your objective is and jot it down on a scrap of paper. If you were to perform a money spell, your objective would be as follows: "I intend to do so become prosperous financially "You may be required to register for certain conventions.

For example, you would record your objective in an enchanted letter set.

Theban or Enochian are two examples. Due to the fact that this is a spell involving money,

would either choose a gold or green scrap of paper or the flame of a the same hue. Consider yourself as you write your objective achieving the desired result.

Consider the numerous ways in which your objective might manifest itself, For instance, receiving a promotion at work. Perhaps it was a debtor Your funds will materialise out of thin air to satisfy their debt.

On the other hand, you might be eligible for a substantial tax refund.check!

After capturing your objective, overlay the paper, concentrating on entire time, your expectation. Certain individuals enjoy reciting a brief spell.

while they are performing this act. It is not necessary for it to be lavish. It is possible.

Utilize a vital resource such as Additional funds should be directed my way; I could use some assistance today.

Additional funds will be paid to me as I earn them.

Allow one of the folded paper's corners to catch fire in the candle's flame to combust. Maintain as much control as possible over the paper (without igniting your fingers) and then store it in a fire-resistant container bowl to independently burn the remainder of the route. Allow to burn out utterly gone. When the flames have died down, discard it rather than retaining it for future use in a spell. By and large, little remains except for a stub of wax, which you may bury or discard.

You may do so in any manner you wish.

Divination Using Candle Magic

Candles are used in divinatory rituals in some mystical traditions.

The two most frequently used techniques for divining with flames are as follows:

Observation of the wax and the manner in which the fire burns.

To make a determination based on the way the fire burns, you must consider whether If a fire burns low or high, if it flashes, or if there are multiple fires, all of these conditions apply. Two Flares may indicate that you are receiving assistance from the spirit world. you will accomplish your goal. Indeed, even the colours emitted by a fire may be a source of confusion.

Regardless, There is no consensus regarding the significance of these symbols. While some individuals Experts agree that a fire that burns tall and steadily indicates one's While some argue that the length and nature of the desire will be satisfied, others point out that A wick, as well as an air vent, can influence how the fire burns. Concentrate on your objective rather than the fire's behaviour.

However, if you require divination via candle wax reading, you will need to place the wax in a bowl of cold water to cool it. Solidification of the wax swiftly and in a variety of shapes. Utilize these shapes to assist you in locating the answers. to your inquiries, much like a tea leaf reader would.

CHAPTER 5:

PSYCHIC ABILITIES, DIVINATION, AND PREDICTING THE FUTURE

This chapter will discuss the additional skills required for practising witchcraft within the Wiccan religion. Again, they are not necessary when attempting to become a witch, but they may pique your interest.

The concept of a witch, or even Wicca, frequently conjures up images of psychics setting up tents at carnivals and claiming to be able to read your future.

While no one is here to debate whether any of those are legitimate, set the record straight by stating that Wiccans are not included in that misinterpretation. Wiccans and witches are individuals who are highly attuned to their intuition and act on it. It is not a matter of waking up and suddenly being able to read minds; it is a matter of applying various practises that will enhance an ability that all human beings are born with. We all have unexplained feelings about things; we refer to these as hunches or gut feelings. Wiccans believe that everyone is born with some degree of psychic ability and that this ability has been either encouraged or discouraged throughout their lives, depending on their culture or upbringing.

ESP attempts to encompass all facets of psychic abilities, including clairvoyance, clairaudience, psychometry, telepathy, dowsing, precognition, scrying, and mediumship. These are not easy-to-access abilities. Certain skills may be superior to others depending on your upbringing. It will take time to bring them to the surface after being pushed down for so long.

Accepting that you are capable of these things is the first step. You can begin by reminding yourself daily with a statement such as "I am receptive and open to information."

Begin by conducting research, whether in other books or on the internet.

Additionally, you must understand that, as with most skills, you will not be proficient in all psychic abilities. Determine your strengths and areas of potential affinity. Accept that the majority of people are extrasensory in only one or two ways and move forward with your investigation of your particular psychic abilities.

Acquiring the Ability to Trust Your Intuition

The majority of Wiccans recommend that you attempt to tune into your abilities by paying attention to your senses rather than blocking them out. This will bring you closer to the present moment.

If you are someone who does not trust their intuition and is conflating their emotions with that sensation, the following are a few ways to clear your mind and develop the ability to trust yourself when making decisions or interpreting events in your life:

1. Begin with a straightforward decision, such as whether to walk or take the bus to work today.

2. One response will occur to you. Keep a record of it. Make no attempt to justify your actions; simply write them down.

3. Inhale and exhale deeply and quietly. Your intuition is the answer that arose in your mind. Without scanning your brain for reasons why or why not, trust that thought.

4. Now make your choice and stick with it. While the outcomes are not always optimal, this does not mean that your intuition was incorrect. We cannot know what did not occur as a result of our choices.

Another exercise can assist you in visualising the concept of following your intuition. This exercise requires you to visualise a traffic light.

1. Clear your mind and schedule some uninterrupted time for yourself. Take a comfortable seat and inhale deeply.

2. When you are ready, jot down some questions about your life that you believe require an answer. In this case, the responses will be yes, no, or possibly.

3. Now take a deep breath and close your eyes. Consider a traffic light with three distinct colours: red, yellow, and green. The green light indicates "yes," the red light indicates "no," and the yellow light indicates "possibly."

4. Begin by posing questions to yourself that you already know the answers to in order to gauge the visualisation. Consider

whether you are sitting (if you are), whether the year you recited is correct, whether you own a pet bird, and so forth. Observe how the corresponding colours come to life in your mind.

5. Now, examine the questions you jotted down. Make an effort not to think too much; simply ask.

6. Whichever colour comes to mind as the answer. That is your intuition communicating with you directly.

Pay Attention to Your Body

Your body can communicate with you regarding decisions you've made, as it is directly connected to your intuition. If you are experiencing anxiety, this could be your intuition warning you. If you are also undecided about a choice, you can consult the traffic light method.

Make a conscious effort to pay attention to your body and stay in tune with how it feels. Initially, try not to interpret too much; rather, simply be aware of it and how it feels.

Dreams

Dreams are an extremely effective method of tuning into your intuition.

This is because when you dream, your subconscious mind takes control of the situation, rather than your conscious mind, which is constantly cluttered with other concerns. Allow your mind to assist you in solving problems; it wants to assist you in determining your future, so try to allow it. Dreams are not always straightforward, which makes them difficult to interpret. Numerous websites exist to assist you in doing just that. Alternatively, you can begin by simply maintaining a dream journal.

This can assist you in identifying possible imagery and occurrence patterns.

Over-analyzing

The analytical mind is intuition's adversary. The Western World is predicated on concepts of logic. If you are the type of person who must analyse every thought and action, learning to trust your intuition will be challenging. If your gut is telling you not to date someone, regardless of whether you believe they are very attractive or whether you believe your parents will approve, try to trust your gut and avoid thinking about why you are having that feeling. Intuition is attempting to guide you down a path that it is already aware of; it is not creating new directions for you to follow. Begin with simple decisions, such as ordering the meal you craved at a restaurant, where to celebrate your birthday, what coffee to order at a cafe, or what pants to wear to work.

Psychometry

This is a type of ESP that some Wiccans employ and which many people find fascinating. This is the capacity to grasp an object and develop an understanding of the individual. It is quite possible that you have experienced this before in some form or fashion. If you have worn something that belonged to your mother or a deceased grandparent, certain energy is being passed down through it. If a person has passed in the clothing or is the previous owner, a profound sense of peace and serenity exists.

You can also obtain feelings about people's first impressions if you touch them or an object that belongs to them. Here is an exercise to assist you in developing this skill:

1. Conduct practise sessions with someone you know and trust. Request that they refrain from telling you about their day. Take their hand in yours and close your eyes, concentrating on their energy.

2. Allow your senses to truly direct you. Become aware of how your body feels, whether it's warmth, cold, ache, or peace.

3. Give meaning to these emotions. The feelings are not always directly related to what is happening with them; for instance, they may be experiencing a sense of discomfort, which could be caused by a variety of factors.

This ability can be advantageous in interpersonal interactions. All you really need is the ability to shake the hand of someone you've just met, whether it's a neighbour, a date, a new friend, one of your partners, or your parents.

Exerting your Psychic Potential

Trusting your intuition is a critical first step in honing your psychic abilities. This enables you to simply trust yourself and your thoughts, rather than over-analyzing and constantly doubting whether you made the correct choice.

Have faith in yourself and the universe; what is meant to be will manifest.

We'll look at additional exercises that will help you develop a stronger connection to your right brain; the side that is innately more creative and spiritual. You've probably heard of these two practises, as they've been popularised by the Western World's mindfulness movement. Mediation and visualisation are magnificent tools that will literally assist you in opening your mind, in a calming and observational manner, as well as a way that stimulates your imagination.

Visualization

Visualization is diametrically opposed to meditation. In therapeutic terms, visualisation is used to assist individuals suffering from severe anxiety and panic in imagining a location or environment that helps them relax.

In terms of mind exercise for the purpose of developing psychic abilities, this entails continuing to use your imagination, but in a situation relevant to your life. This will assist you in exploring additional possibilities in your life outside of what may have been perceived as more 'realistic' and 'practical'. Once you can do this for yourself, the concept of forecasting the future and what happens in it will seem less distant.

1. Similar to meditation, seek out a quiet, comfortable spot to sit or lie down.

2. Before beginning to visualise, bring to mind a specific issue in your life, a desire, or a goal, for example. Select one,

3. Now that you've chosen one, leaf through it and create a story for yourself. You are not supposed to solve the problem here, if that is your intention. However, you are expected to consider all possible outcomes in any given situation.

4. Continue for approximately 15 minutes. This is your world, your narrative; there are no boundaries.

That is all. As with meditation, if you take the time to do this on a regular basis, your brain will become stronger and more receptive to the energies of the future that will come to you.

Scrying

Each psychic has their own set of strengths and weaknesses; some are exceptionally adept at seeing and interpreting images projected onto a reflective or mutable surface. If an image of an elderly witch reading your future in a crystal ball comes to mind, you are on the right track.

A witch or Wiccan who self-identifies as a scryer is someone who is more visual in their forecasting abilities. They occasionally use crystal balls, mirrors, a bowl of water, or even smoke and fire to see visions. These images may appear corny or overly stereotyped, and you would be correct.

Scrying is not something witches acquire overnight. As with everything else, it is a practised and honed skill, with some witches being more adept than others.

If you don't believe you're capable of scrying, consider this. A few years ago, in Germany, a study was conducted to determine how participants would react to sensory deprivation. They were deafened and blinded for an extended period of time. The participants were then asked to report what, if anything, they saw following the deprivation, and many reported visions of future events.

The theory is that when the senses are deprived or limited, images and vision have an easier time entering the right brain. If you want to experiment with this, you can do so similarly to the meditation exercise by finding a quiet, comfortable spot and blocking out both sound and light.

Locate a blank wall on which to focus your gaze. You are not required to stare at it for an extended period of time; you may even allow your eyes to blur. Your eyes will eventually darken due to boredom. This is the time to mentally observe yourself and what you see.

If you so desire, you may purchase a crystal ball from a New Age store. This is preferable to purchasing online, as you cannot feel the weight or texture of the ball if you order it online. As is the case with many other witchcraft-related items, it is believed that the ball will choose you rather than you choosing the ball. Adhere to your gut instincts. After you've acquired your ball, spend time with it in the comfort of your own home. When you first bring it home, sit and meditate with it.

Create a semi-dreamlike state for yourself and then open your eyes to look into the ball. Make them disoriented. Try not to be too concerned with what you see or what you don't see. This is only the start!

According to some crystal ball enthusiasts, it is best to read your ball only during a full moon. However, many people use it whenever they please. As with all Wicca practises, it will depend on you and how you are feeling, as well as what is most suitable for you.

There are numerous other methods to which you can apply scrying if you do not wish to invest in a crystal ball. You can use any screen, from your television to your laptop to your iPhone's blank screen. The entire purpose of scrying is to develop the ability to interpret images in the same way that you see shapes in clouds.

Here's a way to practise with your TV's blank screen:

1. Do not turn off the lights in the room during this practise. You're going to need them to see the screen's reflection.

2. In addition to your television, all you need is a small white candle.

3. Begin by reciting the following line in front of your television: "I give light to the technology born, to show me the way, my own inner light." Thus shall it be." This information can be recorded in your Book of Shadows for future reference.

4. Place the white candle in front of the television. Ascertain that the candle illuminates the screen.

5. Allow yourself to daydream while staring at the blank television screen.

6. In your mind, ask the television questions about anything that is significant to you; whether it is your love life, career, family, or anything else. The answer should be revealed to you within about ten minutes.

How you interpret your visions is straightforward; it is entirely up to you. There is no definitive answer to the meaning of a particular image, as different images elicit varying emotions and associations in different people. A guitar image may bring joy to one person while eliciting negative memories in another. Consider how the image makes you feel and the associations that arise as a result. Keep a record of them in your Book of Shadows and observe how the visions evolve over time.

You can refer to some colour references if your visions are dominated by a particular shade. These hues may portend what is to come:

White symbolises protection and positive energy.

Red indicates danger.

Orange: Indignation

Yellow: Difficult times ahead

Blue indicates success.

Happiness and health are associated with the colour green.

Negative energy in black/grey

If an image is difficult to discern, it may refer to either the distant past or the distant future. If the image is crystal clear, it may indicate that something is about to occur sooner rather than later.

Remote Message Receiving: Clairvoyants and Others with Extrasensory Perception

Certain psychic abilities fall under this category because they involve the ability to receive messages from others, whether intentionally and with practise, or without the individual's consent. Read the definitions and consider which ones you feel most connected to as a development witch or Wiccan:

Clairvoyants: They experience visions while meditating, sleeping, or simply going about their daily lives.

Clairaudients: These individuals have the ability to hear things that others cannot. These could be the voices of spirit guides or messages from other deceased spirits.

Clairalients are individuals who have the ability to smell the spirit world. If your grandparents smoked tobacco, this individual may catch a whiff if the spirit is nearby.

Clairambients are individuals who have the ability to taste what a specific spirit tasted during their lifetime.

Clairsentients: Are capable of assessing and sensing the energy fields surrounding themselves and other people, including animals and plants, and are able to shift these energies as necessary.

Claircognizants: These individuals do not see or hear from the spirit world, but are able to obtain information they would not have obtained otherwise.

While there are methods for honing this skill, the majority of people are born with it from an early age. However, if you identify with any of the above methods of receiving information, continue reading to learn how to develop your Third Eye.

Third Eye

There are seminars available to assist you in honing your skills.

If, however, you are still unsure about which abilities appear to be the most like you, it may be prudent to begin practising in your own home.

A person with a fully developed Third Eye has practised and cultivated their clairvoyant abilities. The Third Eye is a part of the body's Chakra system, which is a network of energy-producing areas on the human body. The Third Eye is located in the sixth chakra, in the centre of the forehead, and is associated with having a strong intuition and understanding of the world.

The first step toward increasing your clairvoyance ability is to ensure that your third-eye Chaka is clear. This can be accomplished with the aid of a blue crystal or gemstone such as kyanite, azurite, or lapis lazuli.

1. Dim the lights, light a few candles, and turn on some music. Anything that makes you feel at ease.

2. Lie down and tap your head with the blue crystal or stone.

3. Take a deep breath through your nose and exhale through your mouth. Breathe as deeply as possible. Carry out this action for thirty to sixty seconds.

4. Concentrate your attention on the area surrounding the crystal. Consider how it expands the space on your forehead. You may feel a sensation of warmth or tingling.

5. When you feel as though the space is completely open, check to see that you are still breathing deeply.

6. Allow your mind to wander and observe what occurs to you. Maintain your focus on that vision, regardless of what it means or why it has come to you.

7. If you feel so inclined, concentrate on your ears and listen for any sounds coming from the other side.

It will take time for you to develop the ability to summon the visions you seek or to see them when others request them. Once your chakras are clear, all you have to do is meditate and try to focus on receiving messages rather than judging them.

Dreaming and Predicting the Future

Everyone dreams, whether or not they recall it. They are wonderful ways to uncover hidden issues or to use your imagination to create new possibilities.

Yes, it is possible to use your dreams to gain insight into the future. In contrast to the conscious mind, where everything is ordered and put in its proper place, dreaming is a place where the subconscious runs wild. Many Wiccans believe that dreams are places where you can travel through multiple dimensions, a phenomenon known as time warping. This allows you to travel into the past, present, and future. This all begins with the concept of dream control.

Dreams can be incredibly surreal or incredibly real. If you dream about betraying your lover, there is almost certainly a reason for it.

You may not have had the desire to do this in waking life, but there may be something unspoken in your relationship that is causing you to dream up something you are afraid will happen.

61

Perhaps you've lost interest in or are less attracted to your partner. Given the possibility that this vision is of the future, it is best to accept it and take the necessary steps to explore your feelings, whether or not they are shared with your partner.

The observe are occasionally referred to as precognitions; dreams we have that may indicate what is to come. Lucid dreaming is the capacity to exert control over one's dreams and, perhaps, to organise one's future through the creation of positive visions of it.

Lucid dreams generally begin similarly to other dreams; it is only once you are already dreaming that you can begin to exert control over them. The following are some general steps you can take to begin attempting to lucid dream:

1. A few days before attempting lucid dreaming, begin by making certain statements to practise becoming aware of yourself. Occasionally, pause and say to yourself, "This is what is happening." I am conscious."

2. Prior to bedtime, establish a reassuring nighttime routine.

Take a hot shower, dress in comfortable pyjamas, wash your sheets to ensure they are fluffy and warm, and anything else that will assist you in drifting off to sleep.

3. As you lie down, concentrate on the bed's support. Attempt to relax every muscle in your body. Slowly and deeply inhale.

4. As you drift off to sleep, repeat this statement to yourself: "I have control over my dreams." I am capable of controlling my dreams." If you want to have a specific dream, tell yourself, "I am going to dream about ."

Once inside your dream, try to tell yourself that you are there and that you are now in control.

Certain individuals use their dreams to boost their self-esteem, self-confidence, or to promote positive outcomes in their lives.

Dreamlike states, such as visualisation, can assist with this as well, as they assist you in accepting something as reality and acting as if it is, which increases the likelihood of bringing this reality about. For instance, if you want to be promoted, you can visualise yourself being promoted and then act accordingly.

In an earlier chapter, you were advised to keep dream journals. They are excellent ways to amplify the positive feelings generated by lucid dreaming and visualisations and carry them forward into waking life. They are beneficial for keeping track of dreams, recurring images, and symbols, as they lay everything out in front of you. When you are going through your journal and come across similar occurrences and visions, you may have a few moments of understanding. Keep a notebook with a pen or pencil next to your bed so you can scribble it down immediately upon waking. This will be easier to do in the moment, as you are unlikely to recall the details later in the morning (if your dreams occur in the middle of the night).

Attempt to jot down details about the night preceding the dream, the dream's mood, and the various themes and occurrences. When you awaken, attempt to remain still for a few moments before sitting up to write down the details. Make an attempt to recall every detail of your dream. Maintain focus on a specific piece of information while you are disoriented, so that you can recall every detail. When you reach the point where you cannot go any further, open your eyes and write in your journal. It is not necessary for it to be coherent at this point, and avoid worrying about spelling or grammar.

The following are some dream interpretations for the most frequently dreamed dreams:

FLYING: Reflects your capabilities and may imply a sense of liberation.

FALLING WITH FEAR: Falling with fear indicates that you feel out of control or insecure. Falling in love enables you to tackle new challenges.

TEST-TAKING: This could indicate that you are having difficulty learning something or that you are insecure about your knowledge.

NAKEDNESS: In your dream, being naked in public indicates that you are feeling vulnerable.

TEETH: Numerous people have dreamed about their teeth falling out. You may be insecure romantically, concerned about your health, or it may be an omen of someone you know's death or illness.

STORMY WEATHER: Anxiety or overwhelm.

CEMETERIES: Dreaming of walking through a cemetery indicates that you are in a state of sadness or fear. Additionally, you may be on the verge of rebirth.

The following are less frequent dreams:

RESTROOMS: Dreaming of going to the bathroom indicates that you either desire more privacy in your daily life or that you actually need to use the restroom and your mind is signalling you to wake up.

GARDENS: A garden of flowers represents love and happiness, whereas a garden of weeds indicates the need to clear your mind of a spiritual ache.

PARTIES: This could indicate that you are making progress toward your objectives.

ABANDONMENT: Dreams of being abandoned frequently indicate the need to let go of ingrained beliefs and habits.

KIDNAPPING: Someone is attempting to control you in your waking life, and you are not pleased.

ACCIDENT: Dreaming about an accident indicates that you are anxious. Almost certainly, there is something in your life that has been causing you anxiety.

ADULTERY: If you dream that you are cheating on your partner, you may be involved in an unpleasant situation in your life, which does not necessarily indicate an affair.

DEATH: Dreaming of your own demise indicates that you are undergoing a life transition.

RUNNING: If you are fleeing from someone in your dream, you are attempting to avoid confronting something in your life. If you are running towards something, you are attempting to attain a specific objective.

RINGS: In dreams, a ring represents loyalty and completeness. A broken ring indicates that someone may be doubting your commitment to them.

Always Exercise Caution When Disseminating News

You bear a grave responsibility for relaying information to others based on your various abilities to see into the future and/or interpret images of potential events. Of course, this is most important when another person may be harmed. The indication that this may occur will not be as obvious as day. You may have a vision of a friend requiring certain medications or experiencing severe back pain. Everything is interpretable, and the more practise you have, the more you will be able to interpret these events.

However, you must exercise caution when relaying information to others.

You may have a vision of a car accident, for example. You then advise your friend not to drive their car that day; they do, and nothing happens. You may be misreading your vision, which is perfectly normal. It occurs. However, when and how you choose to inform others about visions, particularly when they involve potential harm, must be done with care and caution. If you're unsure whether or not to inform a friend about something you believe will harm them, consult another witch or someone else close to you.

CHAPTER 6:

HEALING SPELLS

Similar to protection spells, there are numerous spells devoted to the healing and improvement of the human body. As a powerful conduit for witchcraft and magic, the value of good health in Wicca is frequently overlooked, which is why the ability to cleanse and heal oneself is critical. As is the case with many medical concerns, witchcraft such as that detailed below is not intended to replace, but rather to supplement, medical advice.

Always follow medical professionals' advice.

A healing spell

This is an excellent spell for those wishing to aid others in their healing process. As a witch or Wicca practitioner, you will frequently discover that a large number of people are interested in the spiritual, energised healing that this form of witchcraft is capable of providing. Due to the mystical power of magic, you can use spells like these to aid in the healing process.

As you and your partner begin to relax, you should notice positive energies and warmth permeating the surrounding space. These could be spirits, goddesses, or whatever your personal brand of Wicca entails. These are the spirits that will assist you in healing. Encourage your patient to begin speaking, expressing the positive aspects of their lives. Encourage them to focus on the positive aspects of their lives, whether it's relationships, their career, or anything else, by bringing these energies to the forefront.

Maintain a positive and happy state of mind in order to elicit these emotions in the patient. Close their eyes and do the same. Along with speaking aloud, the positive aspects and energies should begin to fill the room with a strong healing aura and warmth. Once you are satisfied that these spirits are present and are positive, you should begin encouraging them to assist in the healing process.

Begin quietly, so as not to disturb your patient, by listing the issues that are troubling the patient and on which you wish the spirits to focus. During this time, the patient should concentrate on the positive aspects of their lives and the activities they enjoy doing when they are feeling their best.

If you have previously practised the protective spells in this book, begin by forming the positive shield with an aura of light. Rather than limiting this to self-protection, visualise the light reaching out from beyond you and coating the patient. Not only will this healing energy be able to keep negative energies out of your patient, but it will also assist in removing any negative aspects that may be impeding the healing process.

Proceed in this manner. You and your patient should both feel empowered and protected after five minutes. Due to the layer of positivity that has descended upon both of you and the protective shield that has been created, the spirits that you have invoked should be able to assist you in the healing process.

Once this is completed, begin to rouse both of you from your meditative state. Speak softly and gently reintroduce your patient to the room after they have been cleansed and protected. If necessary, you can repeat this process once a day to ensure that your patient receives the highest quality of positive energy.

Along with this healing process, the patient's interaction with nature is strongly encouraged. It is not uncommon to discover that many of those who heal more slowly than desired have little interaction with nature. This could be as simple as adding a houseplant or two to their home or simply going for a walk in the park.

Propose as many ways as possible for them to strengthen their connection to nature, as this will increase the effectiveness of your own efforts.

A purification ritual with the capacity to heal

Just as cleansing rituals can be used to ward off negative and unwelcome spirits, they can also be used to aid in the removal of similar energies from the body and to aid in the healing process. When you are concerned about an illness or are not feeling well, it is frequently beneficial to ensure that these types of auras are properly cleansed. To do so, follow these steps. You will require the following:

- To burn incense (sage, preferably)
- A solitary candle (ideally silver or grey-colored)

- A light dusting of sea salt
- A chalice or cup of water (tap water is fine)

These items represent the four traditional elements of earth, air, fire, and water, respectively. In a quiet room, place the candle in front of you and light both the candle and the incense. Begin meditating and keep in mind that the more relaxed you are, the more effective the spell will be. This can be a difficult step for those who are ill or feeling under the weather, but being able to temporarily overcome an illness can be extremely rewarding in the long run.

You may begin as soon as you feel sufficiently relaxed.

Cast your hand several times through the smoke as the incense begins to smoulder and the scent fills the room. Allow the smoke to pass over your skin and take note of how the room smells as it fills. While doing so, repeat the following phrase: "I cleanse myself with air."

Following that, place your hand over the burning candle (not too close that it causes pain, but close enough to feel the heat on your palm) and say, "With fire, I cleanse myself."

As you say the words, you will begin to sense the negative energies and illness smouldering and burning. Following that, rub a pinch of sea salt between your forefingers and thumb. Then rub the salt into the palms of both hands and repeat to yourself, "I cleanse myself with earth."

Finally, immerse your hands in water to remove any salt or traces of sage incense. As you wash your hands, repeat these words: "I cleanse myself with water."

Once this is complete, you can extinguish the candles using your still-wet fingers and thoroughly dry your hands. If everything is done correctly, you should begin to notice the illness and negative spirits dissipating over the next few days.

A shamanistic spell for the annihilation of negativity

If you continue to come into contact with negative and harmful energies, this can have a detrimental effect on your health. In these situations, the most effective solution is frequently to simply ask the energies to leave. Wicca's power is such that it will not only assist you in identifying these energies, but will also empower you to properly dismiss them from your life. If this describes your situation, continue reading to learn the best way to address these concerns.

All that is required to complete the exercise is a quiet room and a red candle. All lights should be turned off and the candle should be placed directly in front of you. Begin meditating as soon as it is lit. Rather than closing your eyes, keep them open and focus directly on the flame as it burns. Consider the power and strength of fire as a general force as you consider the lit candle. This is the kind of power that will enable you to expel negativity.

Once you've settled on the concept of the fire, you'll need to speak the following words aloud to the room: "Any energy that is no longer serving me, please leave now."

We appreciate your presence.

Now I am returning you to your home."

The manner in which you say the words will be significant. You'll need to infuse your voice with conviction, focusing on the strength of the fire in front of you and channelling that strength into the tone that will drive out negativity.

71

Repete the words, driving them out into the open space of the room. It can be beneficial to visualise the negativity being expelled from your body, peeling away like the skin of a snake. This is the healing process brought to life, assisting you in identifying the appropriate energy with which to heal yourself and driving out negative energies.

As you progress, you should feel lighter and lighter. Once this sensation begins to manifest, you may extinguish the candle and resume your normal activities while you heal.

A light-based healing spell

We've already discussed how strong light is as a force and how it can be used to clear your life of negative and harmful energies. As the final step for those seeking a healing solution, light may very well be the missing ingredient necessary to achieve the best results. Repairing the holes in your aura with light is critical for those who have completed the healing steps; continue reading to learn how this can be accomplished.

Once again, find a quiet spot to sit and make certain you will not be disturbed. We will repair the holes using the method of aura creation that we discussed previously, beginning with the top of your head. This is one of the most vital areas of the body and will thus require immediate healing. Consider the light on your head as a crown, a symbol of strength affixed to the crown of your head. Maintain this image and reach up and gently touch your head with your fingers.

This requires you to now stretch the healing light down over your body. As the powerful aura spreads across your body, it begins to fill in any gaps or holes that have appeared and may be causing you problems. While doing so, say the following: "I request that my energy body be filled with pure healing light."

Repeat these words several times until you are confident that the healing process has been carried out properly and your aura has been repaired. Once completed, express gratitude to the spirits, goddess, and elements, and return to your normal life. If you have been feeling ill, it may be beneficial to repeat this process several times to help you repair yourself more effectively while you are feeling your worst.

A self-healing incantation

As important as an awareness of Wicca's power is, using it on yourself can be an excellent way to heal general malaise and worry about your person. For this incantation, you will be utilising ancient wisdom to maximise the healing properties inherent in Wicca.

More than any other spell, this powerful one is entirely dependent on the witch's abilities. Even if you consider yourself to be a novice, practising and perfecting this spell is critical if you wish to use Wicca for self-healing. Additionally, it works best when combined with modern medicine, amplifying the effectiveness of the medications that your doctor is able to provide.

The first thing we must master is this mantra. This collection of words has been passed down through the generations and has become well-known among many Wiccans as one of the most effective ways to heal the body. Consider the following phrases:

May you hear this wish, Sources of Life and Light of the day and of the Earth, I invoke you here to heal my body and mind.

Learn them by heart and use them whenever you are not feeling your best. The words will assist in refocusing your energies and directing the power of Wicca's energies toward aiding in the witch's body's healing.

Restoring balance and tranquillity to an infected space

While it may appear that the body is the most in need of healing when a person is ill, healing spaces can also be beneficial. By infusing a room or home with harmony and peace, you can expedite the healing process and ensure that you have the best possible environment in which to recover.

It can even be used in outside spaces, though the effectiveness might be limited by both the power of the spell caster and the size of the space available. To carry out this incantation, you will require potted plants of the following herbs:

- Rosemary
- Thyme
- Cinnamon

If you cannot get access to these materials, dried herbs and a generic potted plant can be used though they will not be as powerful.

The aim is to transfer the power of the spell into the living plants and to allow them to grow and flourish in the space that needs healing.

First, arrange the potted plants in front of you in a line. If you have just one pot, then place that directly in front of you, making sure that the soil is within reach of both hands. Cast your palms over each of the pots in turn (or over the dried herbs) and say the following words: Balance and harmony, Peacefulness and ease,

By the Power of Three

All turbulence ceases.

As you are saying the blessing, imagine the energies that you are able to generate as they flow into the plants. The living quality of the soil is becoming imbued with the healing energy that you are providing, which will in turn feed into the roots of the plant. Once complete, you should place the potted plant into the space that you wish to heal.

The spell will continue to work as long as the plant remains healthy and alive and as long as there is one person nearby who is able to occasionally reinforce the positive energies which are present. With these two factors, the plant should continue to provide a lasting healing help.

Distance Healing Spell

Our final healing spell is designed for use over longer distances. As you might imagine, projecting your power over a long distance can be more difficult than close quarter's magic. As well as this, discerning the results can be difficult, so do not be dismayed if you are not able to notice immediate results. Persist with the spell, and refine your abilities.

To complete this spell, you will need:

- Three large candles (white)
- A picture or image of the person who is in need of healing (the more recent, the better)
- A single crystal (preferably quartz)
- A selection of incenses of your choosing.

To begin, place the candles in a semi-circle (half-moon) in front of you. The incense should be lit, placed out of sight, and allowed to burn while you conduct the rest of the spell. Take a hold of the image of the patient and gently place it into the centre of the semi-circle so that it is still facing toward you. Place the crystal on top of the picture.

Sit down. Place both of your hands flat against your thighs. Feel your weight moving down through your thighs, legs, and into the ground.

Center your weight so that there is a sense of oneness with the ground and the rest of the earth. Feel the healing energies of Wicca driving through you as you breathe, pulled up as you breathe in and pushed down as you breathe out. This is the process of becoming connected to the world and allowing your abilities to travel over a greater distance.

Once you can feel the powers flowing through you, it is time to direct your energy. Take your hands from your legs and hold them above the crystal. Continue to breathe deeply, moving the energies that you have just found into the crystal and driving them towards the intended patient. The crystal is able to focus the energy and direct across great distances. On occasion, you may find that the crystal heats up and increases in temperature. Do not worry if this is the case. It can often be taken as a good sign, though it is not essential.

As you continue to direct the energy, discover the light of the candles as it is laid out before you. Notice the protective ring that they are able to form and focus this energy again through the crystal. The light that is created by these candles is a healing one, one that you are stretching across a great distance.

Finally, imagine the patient as you wish them to be. Imagine them healthy and well, emboldened by the power of Wicca which you have sent a great distance. If you know they are using medicine, then imagine that the drugs are even more effective and that the positive energies that are sent are coating them in a warm glow.

Once this is done. Place your hands back on your thighs and resume a regular breathing pattern. With the incense still burning, extinguish the candles and remove all of the items. The energy which you have sent is complete, but allow the positive emotions to mix with the smell of the incense as it heals the patient.

CHAPTER 7:

HOW TO ADVANCE YOUR MAGIC

Before we proceed, it should be stated that there is no one-size-fits-all method for creating a magical framework. Your methodology may differ significantly from mine, and that is acceptable. It's also significant that you can create multiple types of magical frameworks.

There are both robust and delicate magical frameworks. Hard magic entails a stringent set of rules outlined in the story that define the parameters of the magic framework.

On the other hand, the story rarely clarifies the parameters of delicate magic; its profundity, impediments, and starting point frequently remain obscure. Magic, on the other hand, is unquestionably not a parallel world-building component. On the range, your magical framework may fall somewhere between hard and delicate magic. In any case, the most important aspect of creating a magical framework is not how it is depicted; it is how it serves your story.

The use of magic in narration creates complications. If your plot includes characters who use magic to resolve those issues, establishing a separate set of rules for your magic framework is the surest way to avoid corrupting your story's contention with created mystical arrangements.

Magic serves more to create a fantastical atmosphere than to explain your story's contention, and there is no compelling reason to detail every nuance of its use and creation. Because the Hobbits did not cast a grandiose spell to destroy the One Ring, the specific parameters of magic had little bearing. If your story is based on a comparative example, a delicate magical framework may be the best choice.

After examining, learning, and practising The Craft for an extended period of time (more years than I can count), you will almost certainly suffer a bend. One that began with straightforward operations and progressed to increasingly perplexing regions before returning to the fundamentals. This time, you can create something truly remarkable without the use of instruments, spells, or bits 'n bounces, because the intensity of magic comes naturally from within you.

There is NO other path to comprehension, which I imagine is significant in any of the pathways. Black magic is an excursion that should be taken at your own pace, without being rushed or rushed. It is not prudent to leap onto your flying broomstick before you can walk. Information and experience require little effort to acquire.

We never stop learning, and I am constantly on the lookout for new avenues to investigate and give a shot. It is an excellent aspect of the agnostic excursion. There are so many branches and territories to investigate.

Stages in the development of a magical structure.

If you're creating a hard magic framework for your story world, I've outlined six basic steps for doing so below.

Assuming, however, that your reality employs subtle magic, you do not need to construct each of these six components. Don't be afraid to take what works best for your story from this guide.

STEP 1: IDENTIFY ITS PURPOSE.

How does magic manifest? What purpose does it serve? What does the user refer to as magic, and what abilities does it bestow?

STEP #2: DETERMINE WHO ITS USERS ARE.

What contributions have magic users made to your story world? Is magic a skill that can be acquired, inherited, or learned? Are there distinct groups of magical practitioners? Is magic available to everyone, or is it reserved for a select few?

STEP #3: DEVELOP AN OVERVIEW OF ITS LIMITATIONS.

Is magic, or the source of its energy, a limited resource in your story world? Could magic be captured or subdued? What effect does using magic have on the user? Is there a ceiling on the supernatural abilities of users? How is it possible to crush a magician?

STEP #4: DETERMINE THE DANGER.

Could magic be used inadvertently or for egotistical ends? Could it be used to injure or humiliate others? What dangers does magic pose to its user, whether legitimately or because its use is despised or resented by society?

STEP #5: INQUIRE ABOUT ITS ORIGIN.

How is magic conjured? How does it acquire this capacity? Is there a variety of types of magic, or did magic expand over time? What significant recorded events occurred in your story world as a result of the use or inability to use magic?

STEP #6: CONSIDER THE CULTURE OF THE ENTITY.

Has magic remained imperceptible in your story's world? If this is true, why? Exist supernatural social hierarchies or a hierarchy of importance for magic users? Is a magic user distinguished by their attire, appearance, or some other distinguishing characteristic? Do magic users have their own language, religion, holidays, and other social identifiers?

Your magic's rules

1. Ingesting originates from a variety of sources and occurrences on a continuous basis

We live in an information age; we can find over a million spells online and a plethora of books on black magic, but the one thing we seem to overlook is that everyone is unique. Learning occurs/comes from a variety of perspectives. We can learn from Nature (as witches of old did), from an instructor or someone more developed than us, from a book, from a friendly conversation with our coven members or companions, from a conversation with a spirit, and from a dream.

When we recognise that we live in a daily reality in which we are both educator and student, we realise that instruction occurs continuously. The more our awareness expands and we examine our lives with open eyes, the more we see what everything reveals: sympathy, perseverance, appreciation, discretion, satisfaction, astuteness, and magic.

2. Determining your personal style

There is a valid reason why we are who we are, and in reality, we chose our identity. The more we discover ourselves, the more we discover how to accomplish tasks in our unique way and respect that mysterious individual way.

There is a legitimate reason why we are acceptable in divination but not in spellcasting, or, more precisely, why we are acceptable in reading tea leaves but not in reading tarot cards. We do what we believe is acceptable, what fulfils us, what makes us feel accomplished, what makes us feel secure, and what alleviates our tension and fear of disappointment. All of these occur intuitively to the greater part of us, but these instruments of our mind are present on a regular basis.

When we challenge ourselves, gaining new useful knowledge, and stepping outside our usual range of familiarity, it takes considerable energy and tolerance to have the option of discovering additional information and feeling great while performing well in it.

3. A sense of orientation

As with any other form of craftsmanship or art that aligns with our intuitive sense of direction, black magic is another way to communicate our identity and purpose for being here. According to a loose translation, Buddha stated, "It takes an entire life to discover your motivation in daily life." The sooner we discover our motivation, the more attuned we are to our inner world, and the easier it is to find ways to honour this reason through our actions and words.

4. Self-Awareness

Our physical structure is the vessel for our mind, and our spirit is the very articulation of the Divine—yet we learn from the start that we are irrationally different from others, that we all have similar requirements, and that we should do as X does.

You have heard the legends and the discourses. They meet their needs; however, we as a collective need to remind ourselves to make an effort to respect ourselves.

Additionally, when I say respect, I mean to express my admiration for you.

Keep a positive attitude and do whatever makes you happy, and this, as perplexing as it may sound, came in the necessary sentence from my gatekeeper heavenly attendant. All you need to do in life is 'Love yourself.' If we can allow that to happen, which we frequently do, we not only transmit magic; we are magic, as we originate from a similar divine power that created everything that is, was, and will be. We are love, and love is awe-inspiring.

5. There is strength in candour.

While complicated spells and rituals undoubtedly have their advantages, have you ever considered why a sincere wish made over a flame or in a dream might work as expected?

Because magic is dynamic and consistent in any case, bolstered by explicit occasions, dates, and magical objects, magic occurs primarily and regularly, sometimes unnoticed like a breeze, but the most mystical instrument is the Witch's-body, psyche, and soul.

At any point where you believe a spell is excessively entangled or does not sound useful to you, you have a valid reason for doing so. To begin, we return to point two: this may not be your style, and if it does not bode well, streamline it. A Witch's spells are similar to an artist's sonnets; while we may admire various artisans, it is ultimately our minds that we seek to communicate through our magic, and this will become our heritage as Witches.

6. Patience is necessary

I was a witch when I was younger, and my grandmother used to tell me to disregard the spell and practise tolerance. She frequently used the accompanying illustration: When you place a blossom bulb beneath the dirt, you do not repeatedly burrow into the earth to check on its development, as this will inevitably destroy the plant.

Rather than that, you deal with it constantly and patiently wait for it to grow and blossom.

I've been practising magic lately, and today I'm looking for RESULTS. It is possible; however, this is not the case in the majority of cases. Normal magic occurs in a predictable manner, and this requires considerable investment.

I recall that I used magic to discover my sister's spirit and worked tirelessly for the next two years. Even though the Universe updated me, this was the situation, and it took two years. Despite the fact that I was requesting a sister spirit, others have scanned for their entire lives and are still awaiting the discovery of their sister spirit. To return to the point, if you wish to be a wise Witch who learns and creates, you should regard yourself and allow time for your practises to develop and grow.

84

7. Whom does meditation cling to? What?

As mentioned previously, we gain from everything, but more often than not, we forget to close our eyes, allow the outside world to soften, and turn our gaze inward. The first step is to determine how to cleanse our brains. Within the void, we discover how to focus on various aspects of ourselves... Does that sound familiar? It is without a doubt called meditation, and there is a valid reason why it was created during that time period is still perfectly healthy. Why? Because it works and is beneficial for developing our abilities using only two necessary tools: our breath and our brain.

All Witches can benefit from meditation, and while a Witch's support may be extraordinary or even a floatation tank, why go that far when you can simply sit back and close your eyes?

Physical hardship can help us learn about ourselves, but it requires persistence (point 6), and the more we understand ourselves on the inside, the more we will understand everything else.

Additionally, advanced meditation techniques can genuinely assist you in performing amazing feats such as astral projection and developing mystic abilities. Therefore, give it a shot, attempt self-study, and it will point you in the right direction.

CHAPTER 8:

HOW TO GET STARTED CORRECTLY

1. The objective is critical.

The goal is central to everything in black magic. It is something you absolutely must understand before performing any type of magic. Black magic is a manifestation of the Law of Attraction.

Positive beliefs attract positive, beneficial encounters, while negative meditations attract negative educational encounters. Due to the law of attraction, if you have a specific desire and focus cheerfully on it, it will be fulfilled.

That is precisely how magic and black magic operate. In magic, your objective is to effect change in the Universe. In any case, this is only the first segment. At that point, you must feel your goal with all of your body's cells. Consider your wish being granted. How does it feel? What does it taste like and smell like? When it is adequate, compose it on paper. Take care when making a statement. If you want it to work, your expectation statement must be a single sentence that uses only the current state in the first person.

Additionally, you should utilise only positive language. Avoid the use of the word «not» or any other negative action word structure. A good example of a decent goal explanation is: «I am certain and strong.»

Once you've deciphered your announcement of expectation, you can perform whatever spell you wish. However, keep in mind that you must genuinely accept your entire reality. If you don't, how can you claim you're doing it for no reason? To summarise, my expectation is based on wishful thinking, wording, and unadulterated resolve. This standard serves as the foundation for a wide variety of black magic.

2. Prioritize Your Intuition Over Everything Else.

I believe it is worth revisiting. Expectation and instinct are inextricably linked in black magic. When assessing another spell or ritual, ask yourself the following question: «does it feel right?» Close your eyes and focus on your internal direction. Continue if it feels right. If you have a bad feeling, immediately stop what you're doing.

Consider how you could modify the spell (or ritual) to make it more personal for you. Proceed at that point if you so desire. It is critical in this case because if you do not feel it, your spell will fail to work.

3. Be familiar with the Threefold Law and the Wiccan Rede.

The Three-Fold Law is an attempt at a similar guideline to the Law of Attraction, which I previously clarified. Garbage in, garbage out. Happiness brings delight, while outrage only adds to the annoyance. What matters is that this law is explicit in its application to black magic. Because we are dealing with a vigorous level in magic, the effects of what we convey will generally increase.

Now, try not to take it too seriously. It is not triple in a scientific sense; rather, it is progressively similar to a general concept. Undoubtedly, an illustrated cast of outrage will generate significantly more indignation. Therefore, if you choose to carry out any type of hex, proceed with caution, as there will be consequences.

Believe me, I've been there.

A word of advice from a neighbour: If you're new to black magic, avoid all forms of it. At the moment, I am not claiming that ALL black magic is malicious. To be completely candid, I believe that the dichotomy between white and black magic is somewhat fabricated. My point is that if you are an amateur, you should wait until you are more experienced before performing hexes and curses, as you will then understand how to manage the downside. There are numerous ways to communicate your desires. It is preferable to be safe than sorry.

In contrast to the Three-fold law, this standard is not concerned with magical standards. The Wiccan rede becomes increasingly reminiscent of a generally sound rule. Without a doubt, it is fundamentally identical to the Golden Rule, which is found in all religions. It implies that you should treat others in the same manner in which you wish to be treated. Regardless of whether black magic is a religion, I recognise the importance of adhering to a code of morals.

It frequently affects both genuine specialists and aspiring specialists and imposters. As I previously stated. You can cast curses and hexes; however, you cannot do so constantly. Magic is a neutral tool that should be treated with respect. Additionally, if, like me, you view black magic as another path to profound development, you will discover that living by this standard is beneficial.

4. Conduct Extensive Research.

Black magic is not limited to the casting of spells. You must read extensively about it in order to become familiar with all of the possible outcomes offered by magic.

Reading something written by someone else is the ideal way to determine what is reasonable to do without encountering any obstacles. There are numerous excellent books available if you're looking for book recommendations.

Even if you do not intend to join a coven, understanding the fundamentals of black magic is extremely beneficial. Additionally, regardless of whether you identify as Wiccan, it's a decent read.

5. Obtain a copy of the Book of Shadows Initially.

In a similar vein, while conducting your examination, I strongly advise you to obtain a Book of Shadows as soon as possible. Your first BOS does not have to be complicated or lavish. A simple scratchpad is ideal. If you begin your grimoire early enough, you will be able to begin reporting your excursions immediately. You'll then have the option of returning to determine what works and what doesn't.

It will save you considerable time later on if you need to familiarise yourself with the Book of Shadows.

6. Conduct extensive testing.

Black magic is not something that can be learned from books. It is a meeting.

You cannot claim to be a witch if you have never performed genuine spells or rituals. Therefore, do not be afraid to try new things. Simply ensure that they are reported. Additionally, in every case, before testing an interval that you found online, double-check that it feels right to you.

As I previously stated, your instinct is your best guide.

7. **Benefit from the experience of more seasoned witches.**

Additionally, if you feel compelled to attempt black magic but are unsure about making the commitment, check to see if there are any clear rituals in your general vicinity. Additionally, they frequently include covens, black magic schools, and supernatural stores. Proceed to them and observe. Take note of how it feels and the performance of the consecrated minister or priestess.

8. You Are Not Required to Possess All Witchcraft Tools.

Witches are notoriously materialistic. In any case, you do not need to have all the tools and exotic supplies to begin practising black magic. The primary instrument required to practise black magic is yourself, and I'm sure that as a novice witch, you'll find it easier to perform spells and rituals with the aid of specific essential tools.

Instruments assist us in focusing our objective and provide material and visual reference during our training.

Similarly, exercise caution when dealing with premade black magic units. Rather than purchasing a complete kit, you should purchase only what you require for your spells and rituals. For example, if I were casting my first consecrated circle, I would simply purchase a book of shadows, an athame, a cup, a red flame, and a small incense burner with a pack of frankincense incense sticks. Additionally, that is it. Take note that the entirety of this can be found for a couple of dollars at a dollar store. It's a reasonable way to begin practising black magic without spending a fortune.

Prefabricated black magic units can be quite costly. Additionally, you do not select your own items. As a result, they will not function with your energy as if you had chosen them later. Finally, you'll end up purchasing new tools that you prefer, leaving you with two of everything, which can be quite unconventional. Simply purchase what you require for your spells in this manner, and you're done. Along these lines, you'll assemble your raised area step by step, which will save you a significant amount of space and money.

9. Begin with Simple Spells.

Before you can run, you must first learn to walk! Along these lines, before attempting a variety of conjuring and convoluted spells, you should first familiarise yourself with the fundamentals. Here is a brief overview of what I consider to be the fundamentals of black magic.

10. Plan Your Spells and Rituals Extensively.

Prior to performing any spell (particularly your first), make a plan. Utilize a correspondences outline to determine the optimal time to perform your magic. Utilize the energies of the moon, the sun, and the planet to maximise your potential benefit. Choose the hues, herbs, precious stones, and images, as well as all the fixings, that correspond to their imagery. Make everything work in your favour (this is why I stated that you must conduct extensive research). Fortunately, all great black magic books include correspondence graphs, and there are plenty more on the Web, so you won't have any difficulty locating the data you require.

91

CHAPTER 9:

PRACTICING WITCHCRAFT

You've decided to begin practising Witchcraft. Witchcraft is a very broad term, as there are numerous forms of witchcraft practised throughout the world, varying according to country.

While each type of witchcraft is distinct, it is critical to keep certain points in mind before beginning to practise witchcraft.

The first step is to select the type of witchcraft that you wish to practise. There are over 60 types of witchcraft practised worldwide, or you may be interested in witchcraft practises indigenous to your country. Begin by researching various forms of witchcraft and deciding which one you want to practise. While those interested in botany may wish to become Floral Witches, those who appreciate all aspects of nature may wish to become Animists, who are in tune with all living things on the planet. It is critical to exercise caution when practising witchcraft, depending on your location, as some countries still consider it to be unacceptable, and you could face serious consequences if caught.

Once you've decided on the type of witchcraft you want to practise, be certain you're practising with the proper intent. Making a choice is only the first step toward practising witchcraft. It is critical that you intend to use all of the cells in your body to cast magic in order to manifest a change in the universe. Consider your wish being granted following the casting of the spell. What does it feel like? Is this a strong emotion? Use only positive language to describe the magic's intention; otherwise, the energy will dwindle and your intention to cast will fail.

When practising any form of witchcraft, intuition is critical. While casting a spell or participating in a ritual that you have created, ask yourself a critical question: does it feel right? As you cast, close your eyes and delve deeply into your own conscience. Is the spell you're casting giving you a good feeling?

Or do you feel as if you have a pit in your stomach? Continue casting the spell if it feels right. However, if you have a sense that something is wrong, immediately stop. This is not to say that the spell will fail; rather, it refers to the fact that the spell may not work at all if it does not feel right. Return to your spell and see if you can alter it in any way to ensure that it succeeds by attuning it to your own personal energy. Remember, if you don't believe it will work, it almost certainly will not.

One thing that anyone beginning to practise witchcraft should understand is the critical nature of research. If you are truly committed to becoming a witch, you must be willing to study and study diligently. Witchcraft is not solely about casting spells; there are numerous aspects to it that will benefit your journey as a witch.

Reading about the type of witchcraft you're studying is an excellent way to develop a strong connection to the practise. Numerous witches recommend that you read any books written by other witches who practise the same witchcraft as you in order to learn how they got their start and developed as witches. If you believe you are incapable of studying the practise, you may wish to reconsider whether witchcraft is truly for you.

Experimentation is critical when developing the skills necessary to become a witch.

While it is critical to conduct extensive research into the craft, you will not learn everything by simply reading a book. Witchcraft is a skill that is best honed through practise of spells and rituals. Never be afraid to experiment with new things you discover, and if they work well, make a note of them in the notebook you should keep for any witchcraft-related research. Before attempting anything, make certain that the spell or ritual feels right for you. As previously stated, intuition is critical.

You'd be surprised at how many people you come across on a daily basis who are actually witches. Whether it's your next-door neighbour or the waitress at a restaurant, anyone has the potential to become a witch in any form of witchcraft. Communicating with more experienced witches in your area is one of the best ways to learn about witchcraft and how to practise your chosen kind. Investigate whether there are any covens or circles of witches in your area that practise a similar form of witchcraft to yours. If you're still on the fence about committing to the craft, check to see if there are any public ritual gatherings. Follow along and observe how it affects you. The best way to determine whether something is right for you is to observe it being performed in front of you and observing how it affects you. After the ritual, if you have any questions about certain parts, be sure to address them to the high priest or priestess.

Nothing in witchcraft is accomplished simply by uttering the spell. When it comes to casting spells, tools and materials are critical. However, you will not need to purchase everything available when you first begin. Begin by purchasing only the materials necessary for your spells, such as a few candles, an incense burner, and any other materials you believe you require, but avoid going overboard. Beginning with the fundamentals is an excellent way to get started in witchcraft without spending a fortune on tools you may never use. Additionally, several witches advise against purchasing premade witchcraft kits. They may contain a lot of material, but you may not use even half of it.

Performing a ritual or a spell requires considerable time and effort; it is not something that can be done on a whim. When preparing to perform either of these tasks, it is critical to plan thoroughly.

Select the appropriate colours that correspond to the appropriate symbolism for your spell or ritual. Utilize natural energy sources such as the sun, moon, or even the earth to your advantage. This is why extensive research is necessary to ensure that everything works in your favour when performing a spell or ritual. If you're unsure what to use, many witchcraft books contain correspondence charts that will assist you in selecting the proper materials and energies. If you are unable to locate a book, the internet contains numerous useful websites that contain the same information.

Certain schools of witchcraft believe in keeping a book of shadows to record all of their magical activities. While some believe their book of shadows is simply a journal dedicated to their works, some forms of witchcraft believe it is a sacred document in their possession. Typical subjects for your book of shadows include spells you've learned or created, sacred texts you've discovered, and prayers to your chosen god or goddess. Certain schools of witchcraft will record their elixirs, oil blends, and incense recipes. Witches of kitchen witchcraft will use their book of shadows to record their cooking recipes, as well as the magical properties of their kitchen ingredients. It's critical to remember that you can use literally anything as your book of shadows, whether it's a scrapbook or a simple notebook. If you'd rather use a digital method, several witches have been known to use a secret Pinterest board or even just a Microsoft Word document to keep track of their discoveries.

Keep it well organised, perhaps with separate books for different subjects. It is impossible to go over your findings if your work is scattered across multiple locations. Create a table of contents for your book and jot down numbers in the corners of the pages to indicate where you can find the information you're looking for.

Finally, there is one piece of advice that applies to every aspect of learning how to practise witchcraft: practise makes perfect. If you don't persevere and practise to the best of your ability, you'll never learn what works and what doesn't. It is critical that you are not afraid to experiment with whatever you feel like when it comes to witchcraft. As long as you remain true to your intentions, nothing negative will occur (unless you are attempting black magic).

When practising witchcraft, always rely on your intuition. If something feels incorrect, alter it. Adhere to what feels right.

A manual for the creation of spells

When it comes to witchcraft, spell creation is a very personal experience. While some witches will use spells found online, the majority, if not all, will create their own. It may sound strange, but there is a reason for it. Spells are unique to each caster because they are powered by the energies you generate and are specifically written to utilise your own energies. There are, however, several steps to follow when creating your own spells to cast.

The first step is to mentally prepare for the spell's creation. You cannot create the spell unless you are in the proper mindset and equipped to do so. The tools required are extremely simple: a pen and paper, as well as some books for studying your chosen witchcraft. Other witches may choose to harness the creative forces through the use of an altar or the creation of a dish of materials believed to contain powerful energies.

Others use invigorating scents such as a burning lilac candle or a cup of chamomile tea to unwind and clear their minds so they can concentrate on crafting a potent spell.

After successfully preparing for the creation of your own spell, choose the type of spell you wish to create. You can create spells for a variety of different purposes, such as achieving success in a particular project or developing a relationship with someone. Concentrate all of your energies on creating this spell, and use positive language when writing it to ensure its success. Using negative words while writing a spell can actually deplete the energy required to make it work, so it's critical to charge the spell with positive language to ensure that it works.

After deciding on the spell you're going to create and directing your energy toward it, it's time to begin writing it down.

When writing the spell, use words that feel right to you, as the spell will be more effective if the words have a strong connection to your energies. Keep in mind to use positive language to maximise the effectiveness of your message. Some may wonder why it is preferable to write your spell with a pen and paper rather than typing it on a laptop. Certain witches believe that allowing your intentions to flow through you and onto the paper via the pen strengthens your spell, which a laptop and word processor cannot do. Writing a spell can be accomplished in a variety of ways, as the process has evolved over the centuries since witchcraft became popular. If your spell has straightforward intentions, you may not need to write it in sophisticated language. Once you've nailed down the concepts, you can begin to experiment with the language. Make certain to use image-rich words so that you can easily visualise the spell in your mind as you cast it. Some witches consider writing the spell's actions directly into it; for example, 'light the incense' could be written down and included in the spell.

Once you've captured the words on paper for less formal spell work, you're ready to assemble your materials and work the spell. You may wish to rehearse the steps once or twice for a formal ritual, or for a setting that includes a significant event or additional people.

Consider committing the words to memory as well. While memorising words is not required, when you do, you internalise them, allowing them to enter your unconscious and gain additional power. Additionally, not having to read from a piece of paper allows you to observe and participate in the entire process, which adds to your enjoyment.

Following the casting of the spell, a critical step occurs: the evaluation process. As soon as possible, sit down and make notes on how well the process worked. Did everything go according to plan? Would you alter anything about the spell if you repeated it to make it more effective for yourself? After you've completed your notes, file them away for future reference. Certain witches advise against discussing newly created spells until a specified period of time has passed, believing that doing so will release some of the spell's contained power, thereby weakening its strength. Adhere to these traditions to the extent that your own practises require it, but conduct your own written evaluation. Re-visit it after some time has passed, adding a note about how well the spell worked over the course of several weeks or months.

As with any spell or ritual, once your cast is complete, wipe away all traces of the process. Dispose of materials properly. This could be accomplished by burning them, burying them in the ground, or dissolving them in water, among other methods. Clean and store your magical and writing tools, replacing any items that have been used with new ones for the next cast.

Some have considered cleansing their writing instruments with water, while others prefer to pass them over a candle flame or rub them with a stone to imbue them with the earth's elemental powers.

Certain witches believe that creating a writer's talisman prior to creating a new spell will assist you in the process of empowerment.

They will incorporate materials and fabrics that symbolise strong creative and grounding abilities, such as citrine or hematite. Once secured, they will hold the talisman in their hands and visualise the talisman's energy pouring into them, inspiring them to write their spells with ease.

You've now successfully written your own spell, and you're probably quite proud of yourself. Writing a spell is a difficult task, and each spell is unique to its caster. The more you write, the easier it will become. Numerous authors recommend drawing inspiration from a variety of sources, including listening to evocative music, writing at dawn or dusk, working near a candle or a log fire, or surrounding yourself with a comforting scent. Whatever method works best for you, put it into practise and you will never be at a loss for words when writing new spells.

CONCLUSION

The path to becoming a Witch is lengthy. There are numerous things that you will discover. However, one of the most critical points to remember is to disregard stereotypes, particularly if those stereotypes paint Witches in a negative light. Witches have historically been a peaceful people. They have always been concerned with the community in which they have lived and the people who live there.

Remember the ritual described in a previous chapter, in which they walk around a field with broomsticks and pitchforks? This ritual is performed not only to benefit their own crops but also to benefit the crops of others.

Witches have frequently gone to great lengths to learn medicine in order to cure a disease or illness in their community, village, or town. The churches frequently relied on superstition to solve problems. When the issue did not resolve, they would point the finger at the individual and his or her lack of faith.

Witches specialised in curing people through the use of remedies they discovered or learned from others. However, the church recognised that allowing Witches to continue healing people would erode the public's faith in the church.

You are probably aware of what happened next and the extent to which Witches were persecuted.

However, the lesson here is that Witchcraft is a religion founded on love, compassion, peace, and joy. While they do have a dark side, they are primarily used for defence. Recognize that the Witch's journey is fruitful. I, for one, wish you much success on your journey. Regardless of the circumstances, I can only wish you this: blessed be.